TEA SHOP WALKS IN NORTH DEVON

Norman Buckley &
June Buckley

Published by Sigma Leisure – an imprint of
Sigma Press, 1 South Oak Lane, Wilmslow, Cheshire SK9 6AR, England.

British Library Cataloguing in Publication Data
A CIP record for this book is available from the British Library.

ISBN: 1-85058-605-5

Typesetting and Design by: Sigma Press, Wilmslow, Cheshire.

Cover: Clovelly (June Buckley)

Maps: Jeremy Semmens

Photographs: Norman Buckley

Printed by: MFP Design & Print

Preface

This is a book that just had to be written as soon as possible after 'Tea Shop Walks in South Devon and Dartmoor', which appeared in June 1997. The well tried and tested combination of a good, but not too taxing walk, with a carefully selected tea shop was so natural and successful in the southern half of the county that it would have been quite wrong and a great shame not to finish the job for Devon as a whole. So, here it is, the blend as before. Thirty walks ranging from one to seven miles in length, with the great variety to be expected from half of a large county which has a superb northern coastline, the western part of Exmoor and the northern fringe of Dartmoor.

Much use is made of the South West Coast Path, in all but two cases using linking paths and lanes to provide a return to the starting point. The rich variety also includes walks within great estates such as Arlington Court and Knightshayes and less spectacular but equally enjoyable rambles across Devon's pleasant and extensive farming country. As would be expected, the valleys of such famous rivers as the Taw, the Torridge and the East Lyn also feature. Just two of the walks are linear, using good local bus services to return to the starting place.

As in previous books in this series, severe scrambling and other difficulties are avoided but this does not mean that all the walks are nothing more than a gentle stroll. In fact, the great majority are more appropriately to be tackled and enjoyed by walkers in boots - proper walking boots, with shaped rigid soles and ankle support.

A feature which it is hoped will be most useful is the initial assessment for each of the thirty, giving the length of the walk, the authors' summary of the type of the walk and places visited, together with advice on car parking and maps. A decision on the suitability or otherwise of any particular walk for any occasion can, thereby, be made at little more than a glance.

In selecting routes, the authors have always had a natural preference for footpaths, bridleways and unsurfaced lanes, using public roads to complete a circuit only when unavoidable. Even then, every effort has been made to use the most minor roads and to avoid deep-cut lanes between high banks, which pose a danger to pedestrians. Many lengths of disused railway line are now available to walkers and cyclists; these have been incorporated into the book wherever appropriate.

With regard to the tea shops which so naturally complement the walks, June Buckley is both a co-author of this book and a member of the Tea Club. June has developed a great deal of expertise during the preparation of these books and any recommended tea shop must provide at least a good pot of tea, with alternatives such as coffee and cold drinks. This provision must be in clean, attractive, premises offering a welcome to walkers and situated on or close to the route of the walk.

The reality is that wide range, flexible, catering is now very common, with 'all day breakfasts' overlapping light savoury lunches and high teas in a large number of premises. There are, however, still specialised tea shops where Earl Grey, Darjeeling, Lapsang Souchong and many others are offered for the delight of the true connoisseur. Likewise, above all in Devon, the traditional and glorious cream tea still reigns supreme. Even in these calorie conscious days few can resist the layers of strawberry jam and clotted cream thickly plastered on newly-baked scones. Long may it be so; this book will help to find some of the best of these tea shops.

For previous 'Tea Shop Walks' books, light hearted attempts have been made by the media to equate the calories consumed per scone with jam and clotted cream with the calories expended in walking a set number of miles. Whatever the arithmetic, the principle of eating rich and rather indulgent food in combination with suitable exercise, as embodied in a 'Tea Shop Walks' book, must surely be right. After all, those with real worries about excess calories can always settle for a cup of tea!

As before, efforts have been made to diversify the refreshment premises collectively referred to as 'tea shops'. Farms and stately homes compliment the traditional English tea shop which, in an area such as North Devon, inevitably provides the majority of premises. Opening hours are given in the text but, as these will obviously be varied from time to time, telephone numbers are given in each case.

The authors have several times debated the optimum position for the tea shop in relation to the walking circuit, any position between half way round and at the end finding favour from time to time. Some walks have a choice of parking place which allows the walker his own preference in this matter. It is, of course, entirely subjective and may well depend on the type and extent of refreshment. A pot of tea part way round must contribute to the enjoyment of the remaining distance. Conversely, a substantial Devon cream tea may provide an apt finish after all the work has been done but be a distinct handicap if several miles remain to be walked. You take your choice!

The initial summary, the selected tea shop and the route of the walk are complimented by a sketch map and by a description. In conjunction with the text, the former is adequate for following the way round without difficulty, although it must be said that an appropriate Ordnance Survey or other good map does, for most walkers, add appreciation of the locality and thereby increase the overall enjoyment.

The description provides a potted version of the historical background of any relevant town(s) and/or village(s), together with features which may be of interest to visitors, either in those towns or villages or encountered along the way. In some cases the authors' rather subjective assessment of the character of a place is included.

Norman & June Buckley

Contents

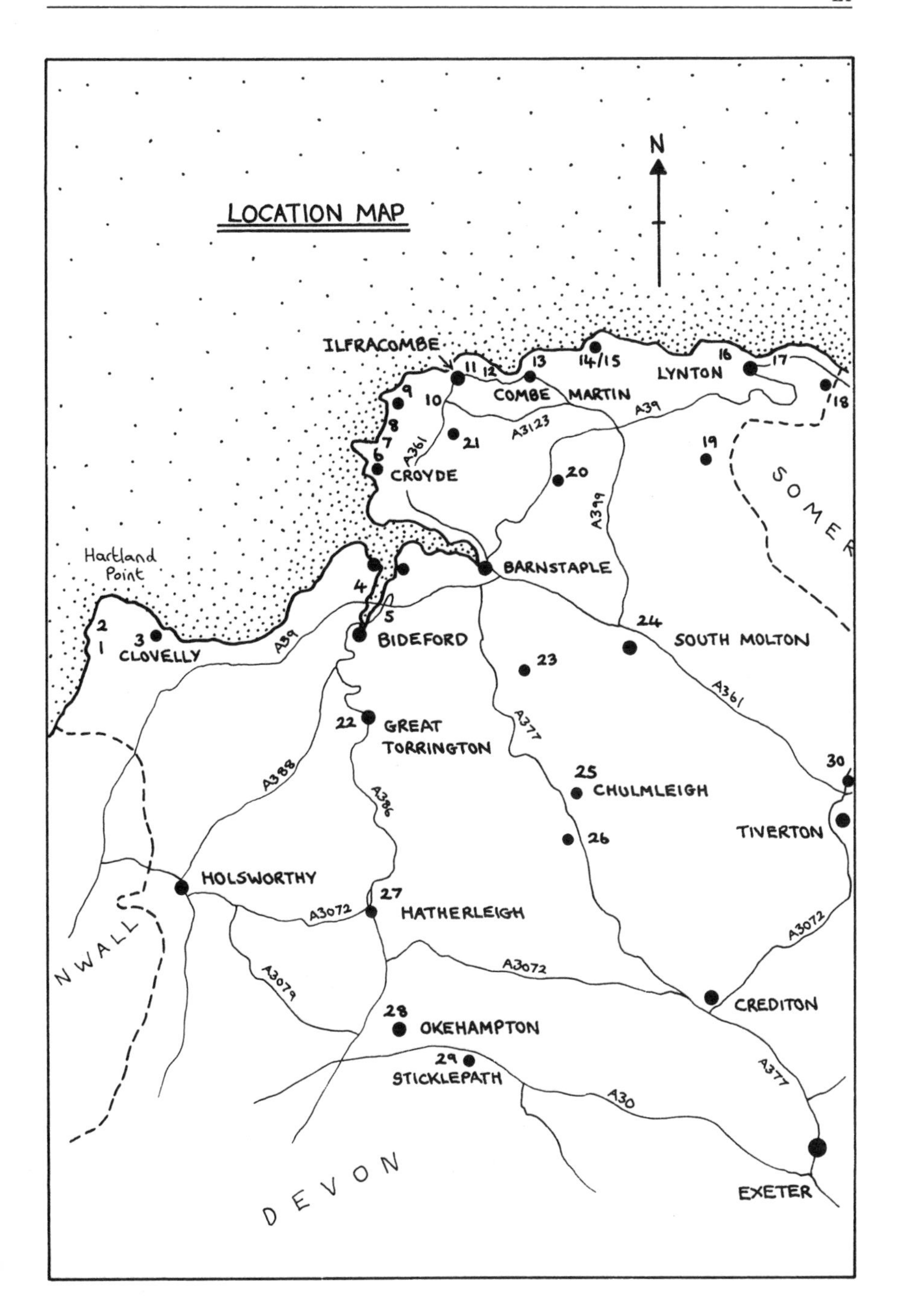
LOCATION MAP
N
ILFRACOMBE
11
12
13
14/15
16
17
18
LYNTON
COMBE MARTIN
10
9
8
7
6
CROYDE
21
A3123
A361
A39
19
20
A399
SOMER
Hartland Point
BARNSTAPLE
4
5
2
1
3
CLOVELLY
A39
BIDEFORD
24
SOUTH MOLTON
23
A361
22
GREAT TORRINGTON
A377
A388
A386
25
CHULMLEIGH
30
TIVERTON
26
HOLSWORTHY
27
HATHERLEIGH
A3072
A3072
A3072
NWALL
A3079
CREDITON
28
OKEHAMPTON
29
STICKLEPATH
A377
A30
EXETER
DEVON

Introduction

The area covered by this book is, broadly, the northern half of the county of Devon. Inevitably, such a division is somewhat arbitrary, particularly as the huge bulk of Dartmoor sits close to the middle of the county and does not lend itself well to partition. Most of Dartmoor which is accessible to walkers and within range of tea shops was included in the companion volume 'Tea Shop Walks in South Devon and Dartmoor', enabling a reasonable east to west line to be drawn a little to the south of Okehampton and just north of Tiverton. Between them, the two books provide comprehensive coverage of this large and beautiful county.

In looking briefly at the history of Devon, at least in the early years, there is no case for attempting to separate into north and south. Indeed, county boundaries themselves obviously have no relevance to the underlying geology or to the movements of hunter/gatherer tribes in pre-historic times. The granite upland mass of Exmoor is split by the Somerset/Devon boundary.

Successive waves of human occupation of what is now Devon are fairly well established. The first real evidence is provided by the flint and bone implements of the Old Stone Age (Palaeolithic) found at Kent's Cavern near Torquay. At that time, 30,000 – 20,000 BC, Britain was still subject to successive ice ages. Although the ice cover may not have reached as far south as Devon, human existence as hunter/gatherers in a tundra-like landscape would be extremely marginal. The transition into the Middle Stone Age (Mesolithic) was concurrent with the final melting of the ice and the consequent development of woodland. Human occupation was still nomadic rather than settled, but a richer variety of animal species was available for hunting. Again, just a few flints provide rather scant evidence in Devon.

The succeeding New Stone Age (Neolithic) brought another wave of incoming occupation from continental Europe, with evidence of settlement sites, in the form of burial chambers, and the start of farming, both cereal growing and the herding of livestock.

The Bronze Age brought the 'Beaker' people with their distinctive pottery and their ability to smelt metal ores. Many identifiable remains, such as barrows on lower ground and cairns, cists, a few stone circles, standing stones and the numerous stone rows on the moors, have been left by Bronze Age people. As the climate was more benign during this age, the high moorland was occupied to a greater extent than before or since and the ruins of the stone foundations of dwellings – 'hut circles' – are widely scattered. The lower slopes of Dartmoor also have evidence of field systems believed to date from the Bronze Age.

The development of techniques of smelting iron ore and thereby producing much superior tools ushered in the Iron Age in the last 1000 or so years BC. In Devon this was very much the age of the hill fort, great defensive earthwork enclosures capping numerous hill tops throughout the county. The ensuing Roman occupation has left little trace in north Devon apart from the remains of two fortlets near the coast.

The Romans departed and the familiar pattern of English history continued, for geographical reasons usually reaching Devon somewhat belatedly. The Saxons pushed westwards in the 7th and 8th centuries, the Danes came and went in the 9th and 10th centuries and the Normans came a year or so after the Battle of Hastings.

Over a long period, the development of farming meant the progressive clearance of woodland, leading towards the landscape which we see today, particularly on the higher ground. The two moors have suffered immense erosion, with the formation of the peat bogs which are such a feature of Dartmoor. High Exmoor has huge areas of ling, with the ever encroaching bracken extending up from the combes. Attempts at arable farming on the moors have met with little success and cattle and sheep form the basis of today's agricultural economy.

Generally outside the area covered by this book, Dartmoor has a long history of mineral extraction, including tin, copper, lead, silver and zinc. The workings and the associated waterways and primitive railway lines have made a significant contribution to the landscape.

More widespread throughout the county, the cloth industry has had a long lasting effect. The extensive population of sheep has ensured that the tucking and fulling mills in almost every valley were kept busy. Many of the structures remain.

The central part of Exmoor was a Royal Hunting Forest, not particularly covered by trees, but an area largely of grass moorland managed for game purposes. There is, however, woodland covering about one eighth of Exmoor, some of it ancient oak more than 400 years old. Coppicing was formerly carried out to provide bark for tanning and timber for ship building. The ancient woodland has been supplemented in the present century by a great deal of conifer planting, largely in the valleys.

The North Devon coastline is long and varied. The eastern end is where Exmoor meets the sea, England's highest coastline with hills rising to well over 305m (1,000ft) above low sea edge cliffs. Although there are some wide sandy bays at places such as Woolacombe and by the Taw/Torridge estuary, and there is quite extensive coastal woodland, the prevailing impression is of a spectacularly rocky coast with the sea pounding against the base of formidable cliffs. Nowhere is this more apparent than in the Hartland area where the Bristol Channel meets the Atlantic Ocean.

The general severity of the coast has limited the human development and activity. At favoured places such as the Taw/Torridge estuary, the area's largest town, Barnstaple, and the small ports of Bideford and Appledore became established, whilst smaller settlements such as Lynmouth and Clovelly have been squeezed into less accommodating situations. Within these limitations, the north has had a share in the county's rich maritime history more readily apparent on the south coast, ranging from making a contribution to Drake's attack on the Spanish Armada to the everyday fishing activity. From the 19th century, tourism has become the major activity. The old port of Ilfracombe became the largest resort on the north coast and new developments produced Woolacombe and Westward Ho! Perhaps fortunately, nowhere in the north has there been the opportunity for a Torbay-like development. The South West Coast Path, a continuous long distance route of about 650 miles, staying as close to the sea as possible from Dorset to Somerset, is a wonderful link along the North Devon coast. The path is well waymarked throughout and a most rewarding walk for those with the necessary time and energy.

Between Dartmoor and the North Coast is a great swathe of rural Devon, stretching from the Cornish to the Somerset boundaries. This is lesser known Devon to the visitors, unspectacular gently rolling farming countryside, with occasional river valleys, notably the Taw and the Torridge, adding variety. This is an area of villages, with small country market towns such as Holsworthy, Hatherleigh and South Molton, few and far between. Although this is by no means prime holiday country, efforts are being made to attract more visitors. For example, the interest created by Henry Williamson's book 'Tarka the Otter' has been heavily exploited, with the creation of the 'Tarka Trail' as a long distance cycleway/footpath following the imaginary route taken by the otter in its wanderings. The last operational passenger railway line in North Devon, the service from Exeter to Barnstaple, has been named the 'Tarka Line'.

Since the early 1950s Dartmoor and Exmoor have been designated National Parks, the former's 365 square miles being mainly outside the scope of this book (refer to our 'Tea Shop Walks in South Devon and Dartmoor'). At 267 square miles, Exmoor is the smallest of our National Parks; roughly one third of this area is in Devon. Such designation is considered to be vital in controlling development in such an environmentally sensitive area and in ensuring that the Park will always be there for people to visit and to enjoy, without losing the special quality of wildness and beauty. In addition to protecting the environment, the National Park Authority has a much more positive role in providing visitor centres and other facilities, guided walks, advisory services, study centre and park rangers.

In view of the immensely varied habitat, it comes as no surprise that North Devon is rich in animal and bird life. Exmoor is famous for its herds of red deer and for the hardy native ponies. Additionally, there are fallow deer and some parts of the moor provide a good habitat for badgers, lizards and adders. Although populations have declined since Williamson's day, there are still otters in favoured places. Moorland birds include wheatears and whinchats, whilst the wooded valleys attract wagtails, dippers, nuthatches, woodpeckers and many others. The coast has a great array of sea birds, including guillemots, razorbills and more than one type of gull.

1. Hartland Quay and Docton Mill

Length: 4 miles.

Summary: A gem of a walk along part of the South West Coast Path, a lovely garden, water mill, tea garden and inland return. First class underfoot, but a fair amount of ascent after Docton Mill.

Car Parking: Two separate car parks above Hartland Quay (payment for entry to the access toll road may be requested). Grid reference 225247.

Map: Ordnance Survey Landranger no. 190, Bude, Clovelly and surrounding area, 1:50,000.

The Tea Shop

As we approached Docton Mill and noticed the "cream teas" sign we were half-way round the walk – perfect timing for refreshment. Assurance has been given that walkers on this route are welcome to call in for sustenance. However, **please** do pay the small entrance charge if you wish to spend time in the garden and/or examine the mill. Indeed, when planning the excursion try to allow time for this extra pleasure. The garden (eight acres) is wonderful and has featured on numerous television gardening programmes. The mill has been restored and the wheel turns - there has been a mill here since Domesday.

Adjacent to the mill house is the tea garden. Some of the tables are on a veranda under an awning and, as the environment is very sheltered, there is no need to be unduly concerned about being out of doors. However, please note – there is no indoor room available.

The menu is quite small but the food is excellent. Sandwiches include rare roast beef, turkey breast with cranberry, cheese with pickle – all served with locally grown salad. Fruit cake, carrot and orange cake, and cream teas are also on the menu. Good crockery and very pleasant service. Open: 10am – 6pm every day from 1st March to 31st October. Tel: 01237 441369

About the area

Many years ago there really was a quay at Hartland, which defied the onslaught of the sea on this harsh coast for more than two centuries. Small craft, skilfully handled, unloaded and took on their cargoes in this unlikely place until the 1890s. Once in disuse, the break up of the quay was rapid and, by the 1920s it had disappeared under the relentless pounding of the waves.

The few buildings at the Quay include a small hotel with bar, formerly a customs house and warehouses, a museum and public conveniences. The Hartland parish church of St Nectan, mostly 15th century but with earlier arcades, is not at the small town of Hartland, as might be expected, but at Stoke village, visited on the course of this walk. The church is a large and impressive structure, set in a

By Hartland Quay

hard landscape. Inside is a late 15th century rood screen, the largest in Devon, interesting bench ends, and wagon roofs.

Along the way to Docton Mill the coast, facing the Atlantic Ocean, is wild and rugged. At Speke's Mill Mouth, the best waterfall on the North Devon coast has a drop of 16.5m (54ft). The old Docton corn mill has been restored and, together with its lovely garden and the tea arrangements, is a great attraction.

The Walk

Behind the highest level car park is a sunken lane with a 'coast path' signpost. Set off towards the sea with masses of thrift on the left hand banking. Join the Hartland Quay access road. ***To visit Hartland Quay, visible below, go down this road and return by the same route.***

Otherwise, continue along the coast path, through a kissing gate. The views along the coast, towards Cornwall, are magnificent and the outward part of the walk is accompanied by the pounding of the ocean. Stay inland of the beautifully-shaped St Catherine's Tor; there is a bed of wild iris by a little stream. Stoke church tower is visible away to the left

Go over a ladder stile at an old bank, rich in wild flowers. Descend to Speke's Mill Mouth and go a few yards extra to see an impressive example of the coastal waterfall, with a bank of ox-eye daisies by its side.

Turn left, inland, along a broad cart track rising gently up the valley. At a three-way signpost stay with the cart track, then stay right at a fork, soon reaching a minor public road. Turn right for less than 100m, then go through a little gate on the left, a side entrance to Docton Mill Gardens.

After refreshment, turn right to go back along the same road to a cross roads. Turn left towards Stoke and Hartland for a long uphill trudge, passing the impressive Trellick entrances. At the top of the hill go straight on into a 'road unsuitable for motors' to reach Wargery. Bear left here, as the road loses its surface. Stoke church tower is in view ahead and the route is entirely obvious, falling then rising to cross a valley with a stream.

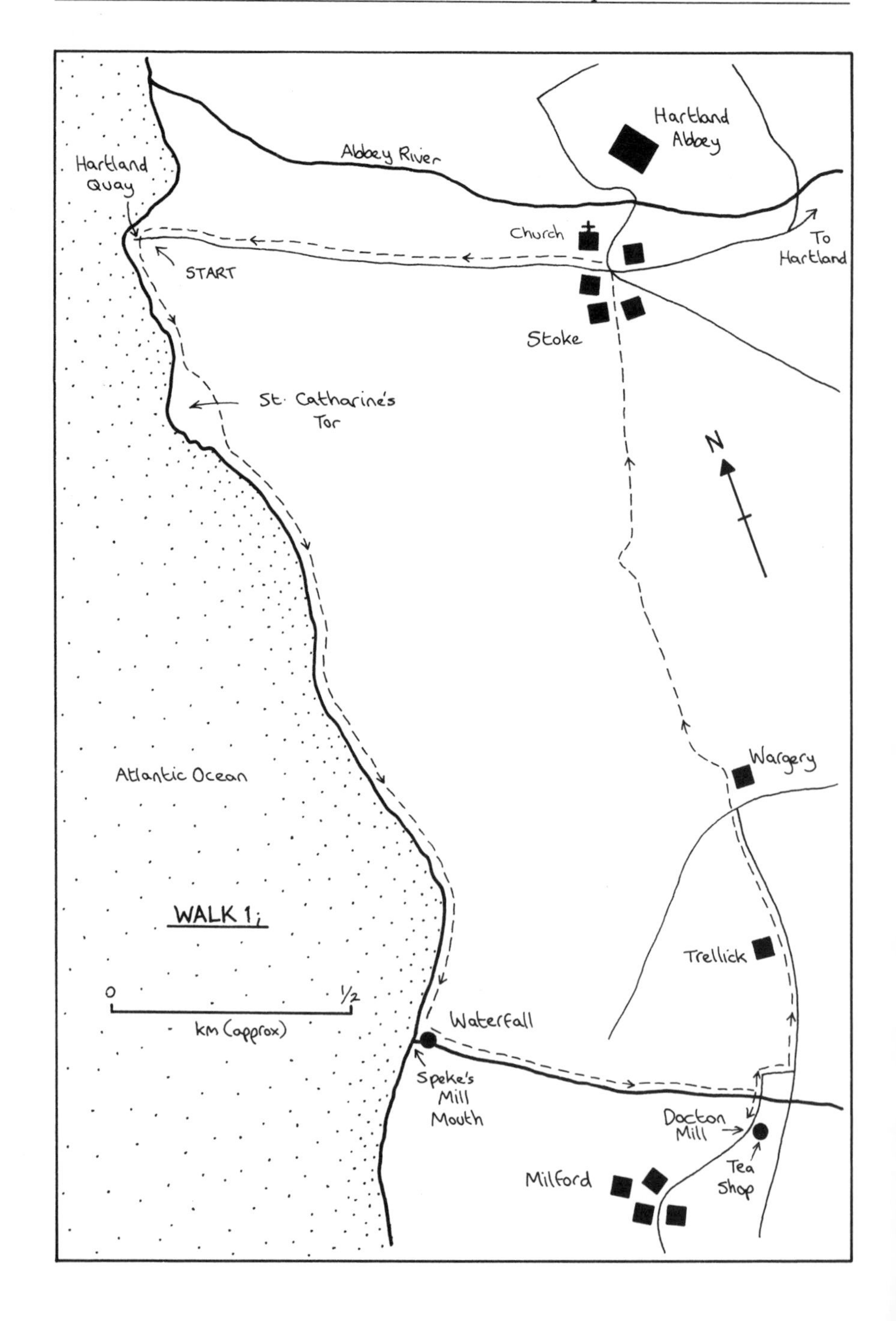
Hartland Abbey
Abbey River
Hartland Quay
Church
To Hartland
START
Stoke
St. Catharine's Tor
N
Atlantic Ocean
Wargery
WALK 1;
Trellick
0
1/2
km (approx)
Waterfall
Speke's Mill Mouth
Docton Mill
Tea Shop
Milford

At a cross roads go ahead along a surfaced road, descending into Stoke village, accompanied by sweet peas, honeysuckle, foxgloves, wild briar, valerian, red campion and others. At the main road, pass the public conveniences and go through the churchyard to a sign-post in the far right corner. The path now goes across the front of a row of cottages, close to the road and over the odd stile and through the odd gate.

On reaching a huge meadow, there is a sudden view down a combe to the sea. Ignore the signposted path and keep to the edge of the field, close to the road. On the top of the hill ahead there is the ruin of an old tower, probably a folly.

The route goes over a stile; stay close to the wall/bank all the way to an isolated building. Turn left through a farm gate and then right along the road to return to the car park.

2. Hartland Point and Stoke

Length: 5¼ miles (8.4km)

Summary: Another prime section of the coast path, starting by the shattered sea cliffs of Hartland Point and weaving its way south to the broad bay at the mouth of The Abbey River, with an inland return via Stoke. About average rise and fall, one or two rather overgrown sections of path, but otherwise fine walking.

Car Parking: Near Hartland Point (payment necessary – access gate closed early in the evening). Grid reference 235275.

Map: Ordnance Survey Landranger no. 190, Bude, Clovelly and surrounding area, 1:50,000.

The Tea Shop

Stoke Barton Farm – there is a special feel about the atmosphere of the farmhouse – very old and little changed. When built, this would be a big and important agricultural holding. It is still very definitely a working farm but has diversified by catering for tourists. As well as teas, visitors can stay for bed and breakfast and there is also a camping field. The setting is glorious. It is so peaceful to sit in the garden for tea. Restricted menu – cream teas, cakes, biscuits, choice of blend of tea, coffee, orange squash or Ribena.

Open: Easter to the end of September at weekends and Bank Holidays (plus Wednesdays in July and August) from 10.30am – 7.30pm. However, there could be some "flexibility" in the opening days – we found it open on an unscheduled day in June! It may be advisable to telephone first if in any doubt. Tel: 01237 441238.

About the area

In terms of coastal geography, Hartland Point is of great significance; it is the point at which the Bristol Channel meets the might of the At-

Tea at Stoke Barton

lantic Ocean and, except in very calm weather, the great waves pound the savage rock of this uncompromising coastline. In view of the obvious danger to shipping, particularly in the days of sailing ships, it seems inevitable that a lighthouse should crown the Point itself. The coast path is at its best hereabouts, weaving and ducking to stay as close to the sea as possible.

Stoke church is described in Walk No.1. The chosen tea shop for this walk is at Stoke Barton Farm, close by the church.

The return route also passes close to Hartland Abbey, founded soon after 1157 and dissolved in 1539. The original buildings have been replaced by a 16th century stately home, itself extensively remodelled in the 18th and 19th centuries. The Abbey gardens are attractive, with peacocks, donkeys and Jacob's sheep. The Abbey is still a lived-in family home but is open to the public on the afternoons of several days (usually Wednesdays, Thursdays, Sundays and Bank Holidays, plus Tuesdays in August). Furnishings, pictures, photographs, porcelain and documents going back to the 12th century may be seen.

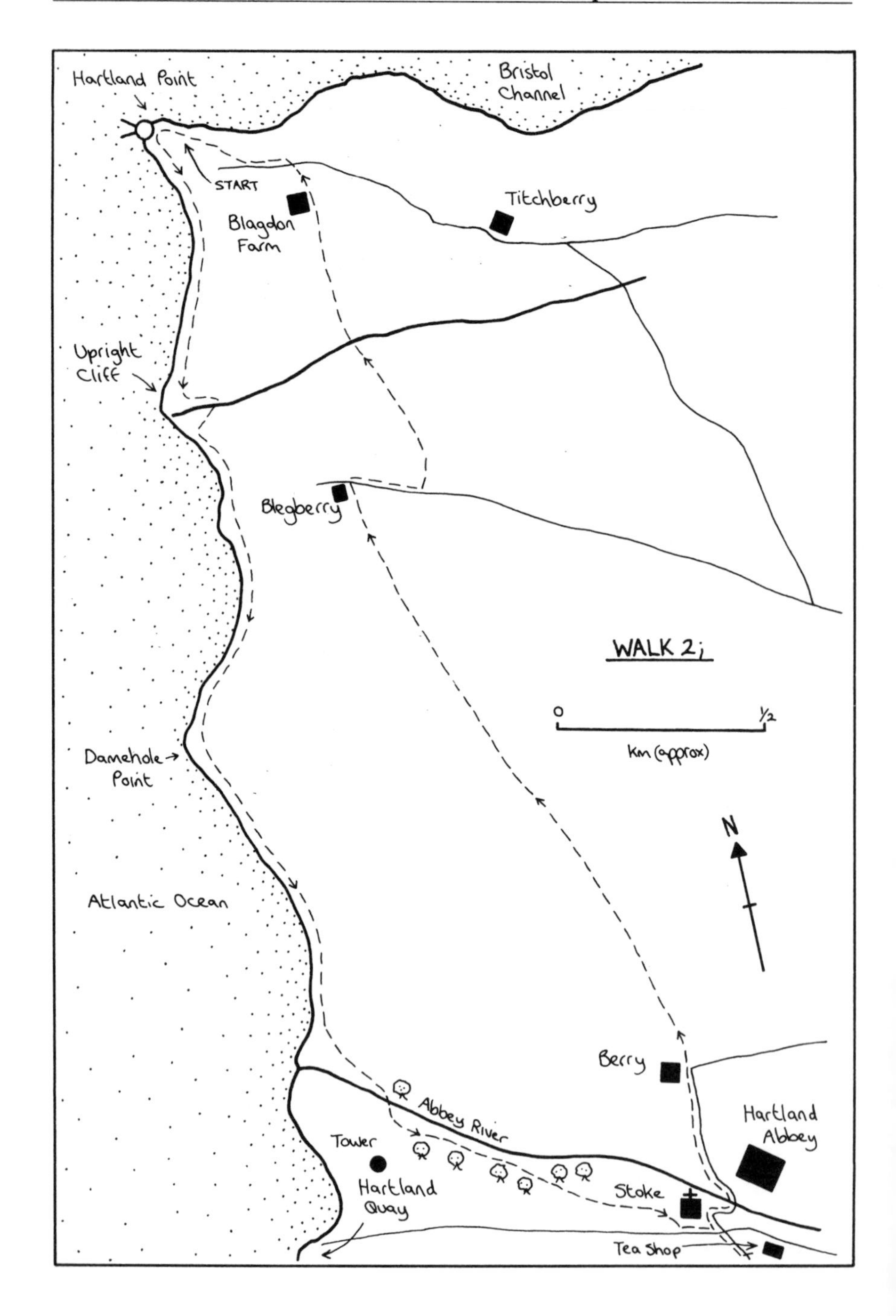
Hartland Point
Bristol Channel
START
Blagdon Farm
Titchberry
Upright Cliff
Blegberry
WALK 2;
0
½
km (approx)
Damehole Point
N
Atlantic Ocean
Berry
Abbey River
Hartland Abbey
Tower
Hartland Quay
Stoke
Tea Shop

The Walk

Walk towards the lighthouse but, immediately before the gate pillars, go left up steps and along a concrete path towards the coastguard lookout station. Follow the signposts to the left of the station, then bear right to continue along the obvious coast path. The path is always easy to follow but is, in part, a little overgrown.

After Upright Cliff drop steeply into a combe with a tumbling stream, bending left to a stile and bridge before climbing the other side. At a three-way signpost stay with 'coast path'. Ahead is a fine triangular hill, a challenge for those with surplus energy. The path by-passes the hill on the inland side.

The ascent of the next peaked coastal rock would need nimble footwork in addition to extra energy. The path turns inland here to climb a rough stony section. Stay with 'coast path' at the signpost at the top. The top few feet of the tower of Stoke church peep across the intervening fields.

The path falls steeply once more to the back of a rock/shingle beach. Pass the cottage in the bottom and turn right at a three-way signpost to cross the Abbey River. Turn left to leave the coast path and follow a well used track rising through woodland, initially beside the river.

Leave the woods and keep to the left side of a large, rising, meadow. Keep right at a waymarked fork to approach a bungalow. Immediately before the road, turn left to follow the waymarked footpath along the front of cottages. Join the road before the church and turn right to Stoke Barton Farm and its tea rooms.

After tea, continue along the road for a short distance, then turn left by the public conveniences to descend a narrow 'unfit for motors' road. Cross the Abbey River and pass the back of the grounds of Hartland Abbey, with Jacob's sheep and raucous peacocks. Climb the opposite side of the valley to Berry, with views back to Stoke.

As the road bends to the right, go straight on into a grassy lane, with the curious modern 'ball' at Hartland Point in sight. The track is between hedge banks, rich in wild flowers. Bear right to pass the huge Blegberry farmstead.

Join a surfaced road and turn right. In a little more than 300m turn left at a 'public bridleway' signpost into another grassy lane, descending between hedgebanks. This track is rather overgrown. Cross a bridge over a stream, join another path by a signpost and turn right to Blagdon Farm and the public road, going straight ahead to the parking area.

3. Clovelly

Length: 4 miles (6.4km)

Summary: A circuit based on the immensely popular coastal village of Clovelly, using the coast path, largely through woodland, to reach the quiet combe at Mouth Mill. The inland return is through more woodland and across farmland owned by the Clovelly Estate. The rise and fall are not excessive and the paths and trackways are very good. One steep section on the descent to Mouth Mill.

Car Parking: Huge car park attached to the Clovelly visitor centre. The entry fee paid per person at the visitor centre includes the cost of car parking. Grid reference 314249.

Map: Ordnance Survey Landranger no. 190, Bude, Clovelly and surrounding area, 1:50,000.

The Tea Shop

As expected, this unique village has many venues for refreshment. The Cottage Tea Rooms are about half-way down the hill on the right. The two rooms are very pleasant but in good weather the favourite place to eat is the sheltered garden. Food offered includes a Devon pasty – fresh from the oven, pork sausage in a crusty roll, or sandwiches, including crab. Choice of teas – Earl Grey, Darjeeling, etc., hot chocolate served with cream, coffee, cold drinks, are all available. Obviously, the menu offers cream teas; a selection of cakes, apple pie, and other tempting items. Service a little slow but pleasant. Open: from Easter to end of September every day 10.30am – 5.30pm. Closed remainder of the year. Tel: 01237 431807.

If preferred, and avoiding the extra walk down and back up the hill, the large dining facility within the reception complex offers an enormous selection of food and beverages. Clean and attractive dining area with counter-self selection. Some tables on a covered balcony with stunning coastal views. Open: 10am – 5.30pm every day all the year except from mid-December to late-February but open for two weeks covering Christmas and New Year (closed Christmas Day). Tel: 01237 431470.

About the area

The visitor honeypot of Clovelly is quite outstanding, a straggling cobbled street falls uncompromisingly down the steep hillside to the picture postcard harbour and the sea and is like nowhere else in Britain. Tight management of the still privately owned Clovelly Estate, which includes the village, has produced a kind of 'time warp' development control, ensuring that flower-strewn cottages and other buildings stay exactly as they were many years ago and exactly as visitors expect to find them.

Motor cars are banned and the hard work of hauling wooden sledges up and down the cobbles was formerly done by donkeys. The animals are now more fortunate, usually being available to give rides to children.

Clovelly

A comprehensive visitor centre has been constructed at the car park; visitors pass through on their way to the village. At the centre are audio-visual displays, restaurant, shops, toilets, picnic area and children's playground. The entrance charge includes admission to several attractions in Clovelly, such as the Charles Kingsley exhibition (his father was rector at Clovelly) and the Fisherman's Cottage, a late 19th century re-creation. There are also shops, pottery, craft gallery, life-boat museum, two inns and the tea shop. Boat trips operate from the quay.

For those daunted by the long return climb, there is a Land Rover service, using a back road, from the quay to the top of the village.

The estate is centred on the old house, Clovelly Court, near the 15th century church. The house has been occupied by the Hamlyn family since 1738.

Mouth Mill is now only a ruin, sitting behind its stony bay at the turning point of the walk.

The Walk

Leave the car park by the access roadway and turn right at the public road. At a junction with a 'coast path' signpost turn left. In 20m go left again through a gate with a 'coast path' signpost. The track is well marked along the bottom edge of a large field, soon angling down into woodland at another signpost. The diversified woodland includes oak and sycamore, with plenty of rhododendrons.

Go through an old kissing gate and continue along the meadow edge before returning to woodland at another kissing gate, soon reaching a stone-built shelter with a seat and with its seaward view largely obstructed by tree growth. Go down steps and through more gates as the path continues.

At a signposted junction keep right on the 'coast path', an estate roadway. In 100m turn right to leave the estate roadway along a way-marked path. The famous 'Angels' Wings' shelter is soon reached, with the beautifully carved 'wings' supporting a shingled roof. Bideford Bay can be seen through the trees.

At the next estate roadway there is an immediate bend to the right to follow a 'coast path' sign through an area of gorse, bracken and

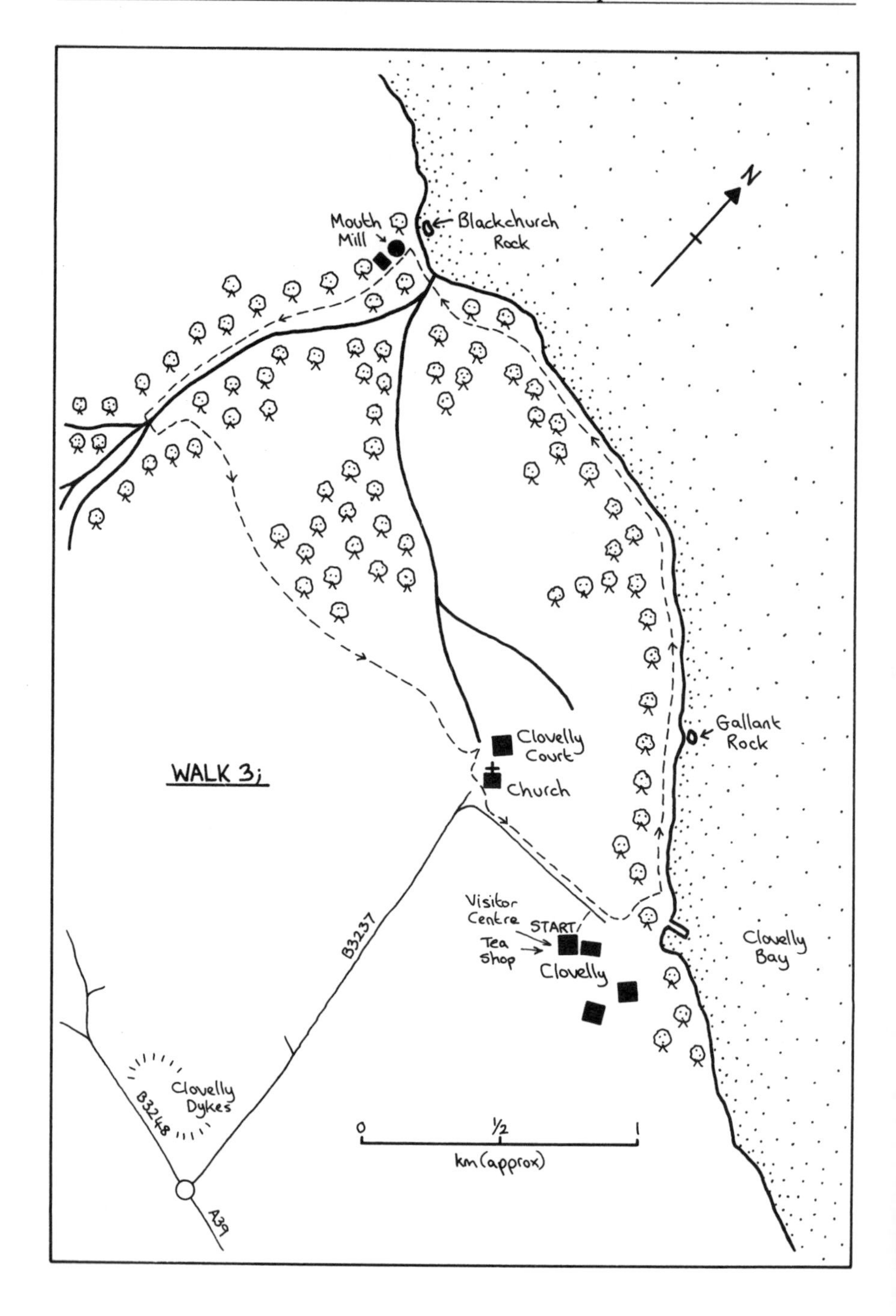
N
Mouth Mill
Blackchurch Rock
Clovelly Court
Church
WALK 3i
Gallant Rock
Visitor Centre
START
Tea shop
Clovelly
Clovelly Bay
B3237
Clovelly Dykes
B3248
A39
0
½
1
km (approx)

bramble. Some sections of the path are very close to the top of what appears to be vertical cliff. As the descent to Mouth Mill is commenced there are wonderful views of coastal scenery ahead. One section here is rather steep and could be slippery in wet weather.

At a junction there is a choice between a permissive path to the right or staying with the main coast path by bending sharp left then right. The shingle beach at Mouth Mill is backed by the ruins of a large lime kiln, the mill and a cottage.

Start the return by staying with the coast path past the ruins. In less than 100m the coast path turns right. Ignore this and follow the broad trail rising gently through largely coniferous woodland, with a fast running stream on the left. Pass one junction of tracks then, at a second junction 200m further, turn left at a 'public bridleway' signpost.

Cross the stream and, at another junction in less than 100m, turn left again. At the next signpost, again in less than 100m turn right, uphill, along an old bridleway. Go through a waymarked gate into more open country, heading for another signpost ahead. From this signpost the Ordnance Survey shows the right of way as going diagonally across the field, but the signpost points along the side of the hedge on the right, reinforced by another signpost in the top corner. By either route, the objective is a farm gate close to the top edge of the belt of woodland ahead.

Go through the gate and along a stony lane, passing through a farm, then along a surfaced road towards Clovelly Court and the church, reaching the public road by the Clovelly Court gates. Turn left to walk on the roadside pavement then fork right, back into the car park.

4. Bideford and Appledore

Length: 3½ miles (5.6km)

Summary: A walk with several differences. Firstly, it is linear and relies on the Appledore to Bideford bus service for the return to Bideford. (Red Bus, half-hourly on weekdays, hourly on Sundays. Stop opposite the Seagate Hotel). Secondly, it is a unique mixture of urban, suburban and rural walking, all on the South West Coast Path, ingeniously strung together by the side of the estuary of the River Torridge. No difficulties apart from a little mud.

Car Parking: Large pay and display car parks at the north end of the quay in Bideford. Grid reference 455270.

Map: Ordnance Survey Landranger no. 180, Barnstaple and Ilfracombe, 1:50,000.

The Tea Shop

The Tea Room in Meeting Street was our choice in Appledore; this village centre café is a pleasant venue. The menu has tempting titles such as: English Lady's Tea – pot of tea, cucumber sandwiches, scones with jam and cream, and a choice of coffee or chocolate sponge cake. Another temptation is the Appledore Ferryman's Tea, comprising a pot of tea, ham sandwich, buttered scone and fruit cake. Other items offered are hot buttered muffins and the unusual scones made with feta cheese, olives, and sun-dried tomatoes. Drinks include hot chocolate and cafétière coffee.

Open: Easter to October, 11am – 5pm; Tuesday to Saturday, and 2pm – 5pm on Sunday. Closed every Monday except Bank Holidays and the peak weeks in summer. Tel: 01237 472589. When closed or out of season, there are other cafés in Appledore or you can wait until returning to Bideford and visit the Burton Art Gallery (see Walk No. 5)

About the area

Bideford is probably the most attractive town in North Devon. From the 13th century it developed as a port and by the 15th century it was one of the busiest in England, later with particular emphasis on tobacco from North America. Sir Richard Grenville was born here and sailed from Bideford to meet the Armada. The long quay has been much widened over the centuries and is still used by a few small trading vessels and by the 'Oldenburg' plying to and from Lundy.

Charles Kingsley

Behind the quay the narrow streets of the old town rise up the hillside; from across the river, with the 'white town' appearance, Bideford could well be mistaken for a continental town, possibly in Brittany. Bridgeland Street has some fine 17th century houses built for merchants and other wealthy townsfolk. The highly regarded pannier market is held in the market hall of 1880 each Tuesday and Saturday.

The Burton Art Gallery and Museum is a modern building with an interesting collection situated at the far end of the quay by the entrance to Victoria Park, where a few cannons taken from Armada ships may be found. Close by is a statue to Charles Kingsley, author of the 'Water Babies' who lived here from 1854. Apart from the tower, St Mary's parish church is a Victorian rebuild; inside is a modern engraved glass screen.

For something like 700 years the approach to Bideford has been across a long bridge (nearly 700ft – 213m) spanning the tidal Torridge. The original wooden bridge was rebuilt in stone around 1500, the differing spans of the 24 arches being said to result from using the timber structure of the old bridge as a framework. The bridge has been widened without spoiling its character. Since 1987 a new, high level, bridge a mile downstream has taken the traffic along the main road to West Devon and North Cornwall, by-passing the old bridge and the town centre.

Closer to the mouth of the River Torridge, Appledore is another attractive but smaller maritime community with a strong shipbuilding tradition, still operational. 'Freeport' status was granted by Queen Elizabeth I in 1588. As in Bideford, there is a long quay, with narrow streets behind.

Beyond the 19th century church an almost separate part of the town with tight little residential yards and its own inns is based on the long and winding Irsha Street.

The Maritime Museum, open daily, is in Oden Road. Other attractions include the Lifeboat Station in Irsha Street, open on weekdays, and various craft and gallery premises.

In season the Instow ferry operates from the quay; one hour cruises are also offered.

The Walk

Leave the car park at the far end through a walkway with a 'coast path' sign, into a small estate of new houses. Bear left at a roundabout to a stony lane with 'footpath only' sign and go under the high-level bridge.

In 200m turn right into a narrow footpath at a 'coast path' signpost to reach the estuary shore. At a meeting place of several drives go straight on, following a waymark, soon reaching a junction. Turn right; the coast path sign here may well be overgrown. In a few metres keep right, by a wall, to return to the side of the estuary and pass

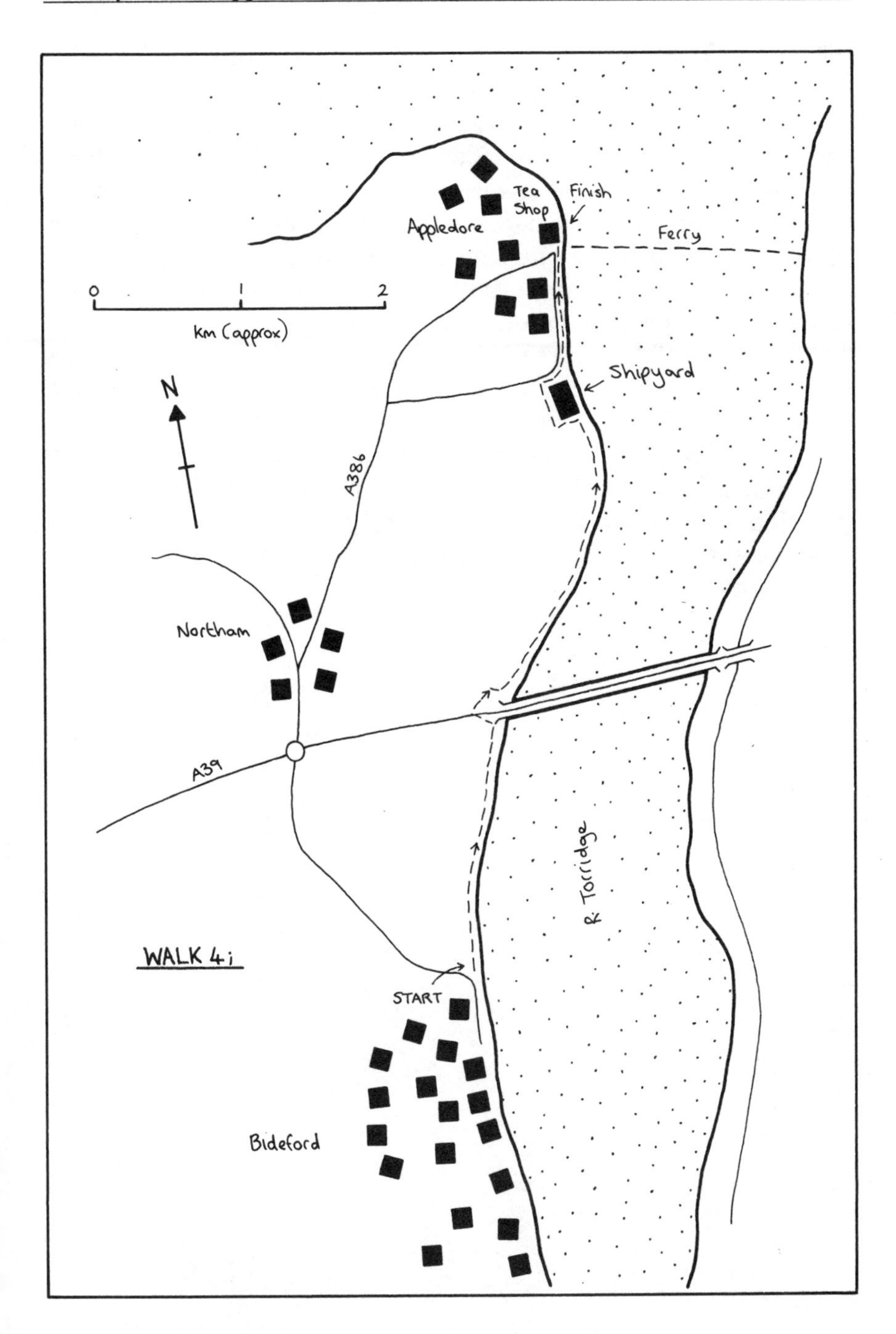
Tea
Shop
Finish
Appledore
Ferry
0
1
2
km (approx)
N
Shipyard
A386
Northam
A39
R Torridge
WALK 4 i
START
Bideford

'National Trust, Burrough Farm' as the path continues quite high above the water and through pleasant woodland.

Descend to cross a tiny cove; depending on the state of the tide there is a choice of route for a few metres here. Leave the N.T. land, turning right to follow an unsurfaced lane downhill. There is soon a choice of high or low tide paths. The former goes left, inland of a sea marsh area, whilst the latter goes along the top of a causeway, a breach in one place being negotiated by steps down and up. Westleigh village is perched on high ground across the estuary.

The paths rejoin close to the unattractive buildings of Appledore Shipbuilders, going left to follow the perimeter fence, muddy in part and rather overgrown. Join a wide highway and turn right to walk into Appledore through the industrial end of an otherwise attractive place. Go along Dockside, pass the Bell Inn and turn right at a road junction with a 'coast path' sign, to reach the quayside. The tea shop is in Meeting Lane, a turning off the far end of the quay, by the side of the Seagate Hotel.

5. Instow and Bideford

Length: 4 miles (6.4km)

Summary: A level linear walk (unless combined with walk 4), on the trackbed of a disused railway line by the side of the estuary of the River Torridge. The frequent bus service is used to return to Instow. Not an exciting walk, but there is much of quiet interest for the botanist and in observing life on the estuary, with views across to Appledore and Bideford. The walking is very easy, on gravel.

Car Parking: Pay and display car park with public conveniences centrally situated by the sea front in Instow. Grid reference 473305

Map: Ordnance Survey Landranger no. 180, Barnstaple and Ilfracombe, 1:50,000.

The Tea Shop

Even allowing for the rich diversity which is always sought in selecting tea shops, the choice of a municipal art gallery must rank as unusual.

The refreshment/restaurant facility at the Burton Gallery is light, bright, and architecturally pleasing. Some paintings from the collection are displayed in the café. Morning coffee is available. From noon – 2.30pm light lunches are served. There is a chilled salad bar for self-selection, sandwiches, quiche, and a choice of hot dishes. During the afternoon, cream teas, cakes, and ices, are served. Well worth a visit at any time of the day.

Open: 10am – 5pm daily June to September incl. and 2pm – 5pm on Sundays. 10am – 4pm daily, October to May incl. and 2pm – 4pm on Sundays. Closed on Mondays except Bank Holidays. Tel: 01237 471948.

About the area

A minor Victorian sea-side resort with sandy beach, Instow faces Appledore across the Torridge estuary. In season a foot ferry plies between the two places and the opportunity to combine this walk with walk No. 4 as a Torridge estuary circular may well appeal. Bideford is described in walk no. 4. East the Water is the minor part of the town at the east end of the famous bridge; Charles Kingsley stayed at the Royal Hotel whilst working on his book 'Westward Ho'.

The railway from Barnstaple to Bideford never crossed the Torridge to reach the main part of the town. In November 1855 a six-mile-long extension from Fremington to a terminus at East the Water was opened. The original station was at Cross Parks, nearly half a mile short of the present station, which was opened in 1872. In 1863 the line became part of the London and South Western Railway (later the Southern Railway) and was later extended to Great Torrington and beyond.

The passenger service was lost in 1965, but the line remained in use for freight until 1982. After closure, the trackbed was converted

Restored railway station, East the Water

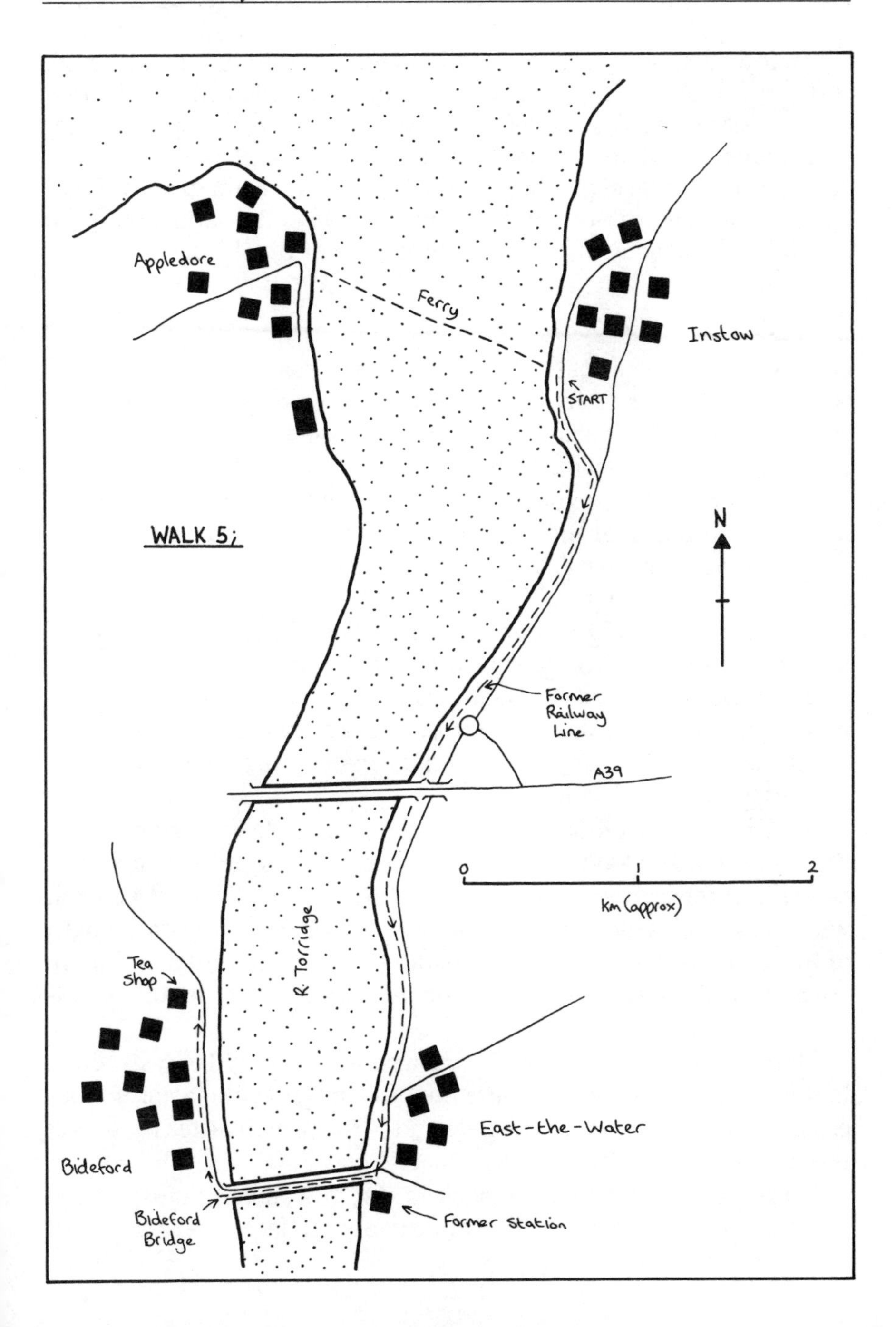

Appledore
Ferry
Instow
START
WALK 5;
N
Former
Railway
Line
A39
0
1
2
km (approx)
R. Torridge
Tea
Shop
East-the-Water
Bideford
Bideford
Bridge
Former Station

into a long distance cycle and walking way, part of the 'Tarka Trail'. Bideford station has been preserved and the Bideford and Instow Railway Group has a number of railway vehicles and a replica signal box, housing a small museum. At Instow the same group has preserved the original signal box. There is free admission to both signal boxes, restricted to Sunday and Bank Holiday afternoons, with the addition of Tuesday afternoons in the case of Bideford.

The Walk

Go left out of the car park, along the Instow sea front road, passing the ferry terminus to reach the former level crossing and the preserved signal box. Turn right along the former railway line, soon passing the North Devon Yacht Club.

Abandoned railway tracks are often noted for varied and interesting plant and animal life; here there is wild briar and a wealth of smaller specimens. No route finding is necessary, but do be alert for cyclists approaching from behind!

The comparatively recent high level Torridge Bridge is a dominant feature of the first part of the walk. Pass under; the ancient, multi-arched, Bideford Bridge, now in view, is a much more harmonious part of the landscape. Across the water at the north end of Bideford a new housing development, well integrated with older property, shows up well.

Pass some smart modern sheltered housing. Red valerian is now the dominant trackside flower. Wayside plaques promise a visitor centre and refreshments. Bideford Station is just a little way ahead, with the vehicles owned by the preservation group on a short length of track. A coach equipped as a visitor centre is included and there are picnic tables. Don't miss the wooden sculpture of a family of railway passengers.

Descend to the road, cross the bridge then turn right to walk along to the far end of the quay, where the Burton Gallery, a tasteful modern building, is situated at the near end of the park. The tea room is at the rear of the building.

To return to Instow walk back to the bus shelters close to the Lundy departure quay and the public conveniences. There are about five departures per hour.

6. Croyde and Lob Hill

Length: 4½ miles (7.2km); shorter version 3½ miles (5.6km)

Summary: A walk with a mixture of South West Coast Path and high-lying farmland. Good views. Quite steep ascent of Lob Hill. Fine underfoot although the right of way across Lob Hill is not clear on the ground.

Car Parking: By the Village Institute in Croyde. Pay and Display. Grid reference 443392.

Map: Ordnance Survey Landranger no. 180, Barnstaple and Ilfracombe area, 1:50,000.

The Tea Shop

May Cottage Tea Room is an absolutely perfect place for tea – a picture-postcard building with thatched roof in a sheltered village. Whilst the interior is most welcoming, on sunny days it is pleasant to sit at a table on the terrace. Service is friendly. Good quality filtered coffee (top-ups offered too), and de-caffeinated coffee is also available. Teas listed include Earl Grey, Darjeeling, and herbal. Meals include smoked haddock pasta with prawns and mushrooms, omelettes, salads with smoked mackerel or cheese – all very tempting after a good walk. The home-made cakes and freshly baked scones served for tea proved to be excellent. Open: 10.30am – 5.30pm every day from mid-March to end of October. Tel: 01271 890005.

About the area

A delightful village in a sheltered situation just inland of the bay of the same name, Croyde is rich in thatched buildings, with colour-washed walls adding to the charm. Refreshment places include an inn and the selected tea shop; there is also a fair selection of shops.

Notable is a small gem and rock museum, open throughout the season.

Lob Hill is not named on the recommended map; it is a rounded hump of grazing land of no great significance but its height of 591 feet (158m) provides a good view point for the great expanse of sands and dunes of Braunton Burrows and Barnstaple (or Bideford) Bay. Croyde Bay, Morte Bay and Woolacombe Sands are also part of the extensive views enjoyed on this walk.

The Walk

From the car park turn right, go straight ahead at the road junction, then turn right by the side of the Billy Budd Inn to follow the well-used track towards the coast. On reaching a surfaced track turn left. The path soon becomes very narrow, heading for a few bungalows.

Turn right at a junction before the bungalows and head for the sea, the path soon becoming sandy. Descend to the beach and bear left. Rise from the beach over rock, by a 'coast path' signpost and continue over more beach to a flight of concrete steps up to another signpost. Turn right to follow the coast path along the top edge of low cliffs. There are good views of Croyde Bay behind and Lundy can be seen out to sea.

By a low rocky headland and a seat, with a first view of Saunton Sands, turn left to rise to the road. Turn left along the road for 100m, cross over, and go up a few steps at another 'coast path' sign. A narrow but well-defined path now keeps above the road, soon widening as it rises gently, with great views across the bay.

Pass behind the flat-roofed Saunton Sands Hotel and descend towards the road. Before reaching the road go over a stile on the left with a 'public footpath' sign. and start the steep climb to Lob Hill on a narrow track. After another stile emerge into a large open field with a three-way signpost to the right, close to ruined cottages.

For the shorter route follow the 'public footpath, Croyde'

To continue the full walk turn right, 'footpath to Saunton Court', pass the cottages and, in a short distance, go gently downhill. Not very far down the hill look out for a footpath on the left, not signposted and not initially marked on the ground. In 50m it becomes

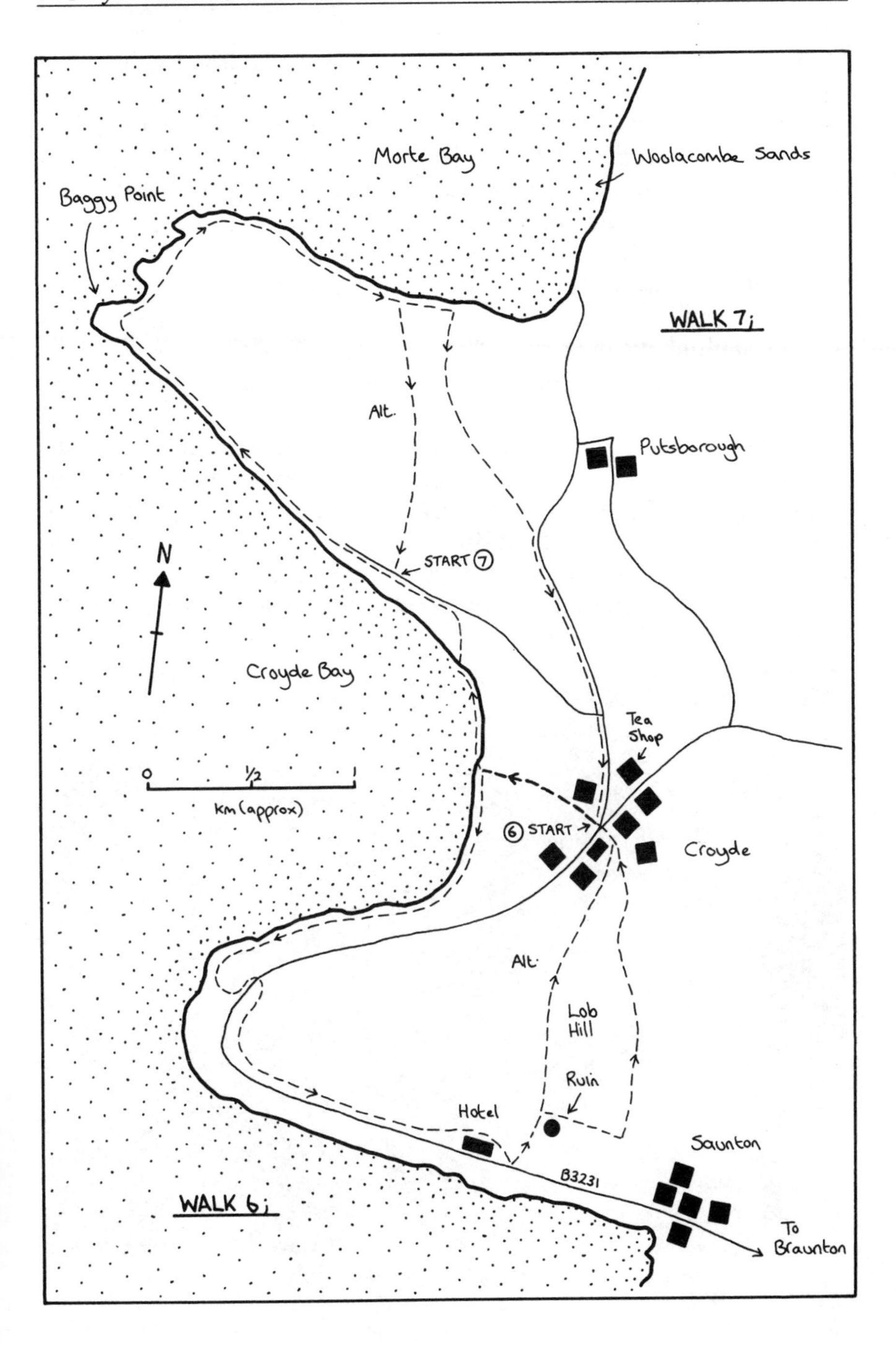

Morte Bay
Woolacombe Sands
Baggy Point
WALK 7;
Alt.
Putsborough
START 7
N
Croyde Bay
Tea Shop
0
1/2
km (approx)
6 START
Croyde
Alt.
Lob Hill
Ruin
Hotel
Saunton
B3231
WALK 6;
To Braunton

obvious as it rises to a gateway. Go over the waymarked stile to the left.

There is no path on the ground; stay close to the fence on the right. Close to the summit of the hill there is a signpost protected by barbed wire, on the left. Angle away from the fence to this post and take the indicated line, descending to a stile. From this top the long views to the north include Morte Point and Woolacombe. Croyde village and an unfortunate static caravan site are also in view.

Carry on over the stile and descend steeply through tall gorse with masses of bluebells in Spring. The way becomes a lane between high hedge banks, possibly muddy in wet weather, soon joining another lane.

Turn left towards Croyde. At a junction bear right, signposted 'public footpath Croyde', still downhill. The lane becomes surfaced, soon approaching the village centre. A right turn into Watery Lane gives the most direct route to the tea shop; if you miss this turning, turn right and then right again in the village centre.

From the tea shop return to the road junction and turn right to the car park at the Village Institute.

Tea Shop, Croyde

7. Croyde and Baggy Point

Length: 5 miles (8km)

Summary: A very fine walk indeed with wonderful coastal scenery. An easy section of the South West Coast Path on cropped grass, an attractive village and a sandy beach return to the car park. No steep ascent.

Car Parking: National Trust Baggy Point car park reached along a cul de sac road to the west from Croyde village. Grid reference 433397. Free to National Trust members.

Map: Ordnance Survey Landranger no. 180, Barnstaple and Ilfracombe area, 1:50,000.

The Tea Shop

See walk 6.

About the area

For Croyde village see walk 6.

Baggy Point has near-vertical cliffs, popular for rock climbing at times when the numerous sea birds are not breeding. In 1915 an unfortunate whale was washed ashore. Some of its bones can still be seen as a wayside monument.

The Walk

For a sketch map, please refer to Walk 6.

From the car park turn right to follow the road towards Baggy Point, rising gently beneath the slopes of Middleborough Hill. Keep left at a fork, slightly downhill, signposted 'footpath to Baggy Point'. By a gate there is a plaque in memory of Henry Williamson, writer, (of 'Tarka the Otter' fame) 1895-1977. Williamson lived at nearby Georgeham and the scenery around Baggy Point helped to inspire his writing.

On a clear day Lundy is now in view, its 400ft (122m) cliffs standing well proud of the intervening 20 miles of sea. The excellent path, fringed by many and varied wild flowers, climbs gently towards the Point, with rock climbing slabs on the left.

From the Point a well-used path climbs initially to a gate by a stony track. Turn left here at a 'coast path' sign and continue, with an old flower-capped Devon wall on the right. The view behind encompasses the whole of Croyde Bay and there is a sudden view of Morte Bay, Morte Point, Woolacombe Sands and village.

At a finger post by a seat there is a right turn giving a short cut back to the car park.

For the full walk stay with the coast path until, at a three-way signpost, there is a right turn along a public footpath. Stay close to the fence/wall on the right to reach a gate/stile. Croyde village is now in view. There is no path on the ground but stay close to the wall on the right to another gate/stile followed by an unsurfaced lane. Turn left

Near Baggy Point

to follow the lane downhill, partly on solid rock. Join a surfaced road and keep straight on to the village, the last few metres being on a footpath specially created to avoid a potentially hazardous section of road.

Go to the junction with the main road and turn left to reach the tea shop.

After refreshments return to the junction. Turn left and then right in 30m by the side of the Billy Budd Inn. The lane soon loses its surface but continues directly towards the sea. On reaching a surfaced track turn right. Turn left into a sandy track immediately before a stream. There is a 'coast path' signpost. In a few metres turn right by another 'coast path' sign, cross a concrete bridge, and walk along the back of the beach.

At the far end of the beach bear left over the rocky foreshore to a few steps heading up to a minor road. *To avoid walking over the rocks, beach exit further to the right may be used.*

In either case, turn left to return to the car park.

8. Woolacombe Down

Length: 3 miles (4.8km)

Summary: A short but entirely enjoyable walk which has one steep ascent First class underfoot with close cropped grass and a little sand and tarmac. Good views.

Car Parking: Several pay and display car parks in Woolacombe. Typical grid reference 458438. Free roadside car parking on the Esplanade.

Map: Ordnance Survey Landranger no. 180, Barnstaple and Ilfracombe area, 1:50,000.

The Tea Shop

At the end of this walk, it wasn't too easy to find a suitable venue for tea in this resort. However, "Normies" proved to be quite a fun-place and is recommended. This is a typical seaside 'caff' but it is smart, clean, with good quality pine furniture and pleasing crockery. Although hot pasties and toasted sandwiches are available, Normies really do specialise in ice cream dishes of every possible combination. Also available are tea, coffee – cappuccino or cafétière – or, for a change, try iced coffee, cakes and scones with jam and cream. Pleasant counter service and reasonable prices.

Open: every day 10am – 5pm (until 8pm in main holiday season) – May to October, closed for the remainder of the year. Tel: 01271 870157

About the area

Woolacombe is a minor seaside resort of Victorian origin, with plenty of shops and cafés catering for its own holiday visitors and for those staying at the numerous camping and caravan sites nearby. It is an unremarkable place in itself but it does have Woolacombe

Morte Bay, Woolacombe

Sands, more than two miles of golden beach, as its crowing glory, together with wide open views of Morte Bay, enclosed between Baggy and Morte Points.

Woolacombe Down rises steeply behind this fine beach to a summit of about 560 feet (171m); the views are well worth the effort which the steep ascent requires.

The Walk

From whichever car park, head south along the minor road towards Georgeham. There is a paved footpath along the side of this road. The road soon rises; about 300m after passing a back of beach complex bear right to leave the road at a 'public bridleway and coast path' signpost. The footpath levels out to provide a delightful route above the fine golden sand.

In about three quarters of a mile there is a choice; left to angle up to Marine Drive, by public conveniences, or right then left to continue much as before. Marine Drive provides perfectly good walking but, if crowded with parked cars, the second option is better. The two routes come back together in a further three-quarters of a mile.

After a National Trust barrier Marine Drive loses its surface and, a little way further, there is no entry for vehicles.

Thirty metres before a 'coast path' signpost turn left, go over a stile and commence the climb to the top of Woolacombe Down, amid thick growing shrubs, carpeted with bluebells in May. Gorse soon takes over as height is gained and the views over Woolacombe to Morte Point are very fine. Behind, Croyde Bay can be seen over the Baggy Point headland.

There is a welcome seat just before the top and the way continues, unmistakable on the ground, along the crest of the Down, with Woolacombe now very much in view below. Although not the prettiest village in Devon, the mixture of Victorian and twentieth century development is not unattractive on a sunny day. There is less to be said for the modern development on the higher ground inland.

Descend steadily towards Potter Hill; either go straight over the top with a steep descent on a bramble-constricted path on the far side, or go left to pass around the little hill. In either case make for a signposted gate at the bottom, go through and continue along the roadside back to your car park.

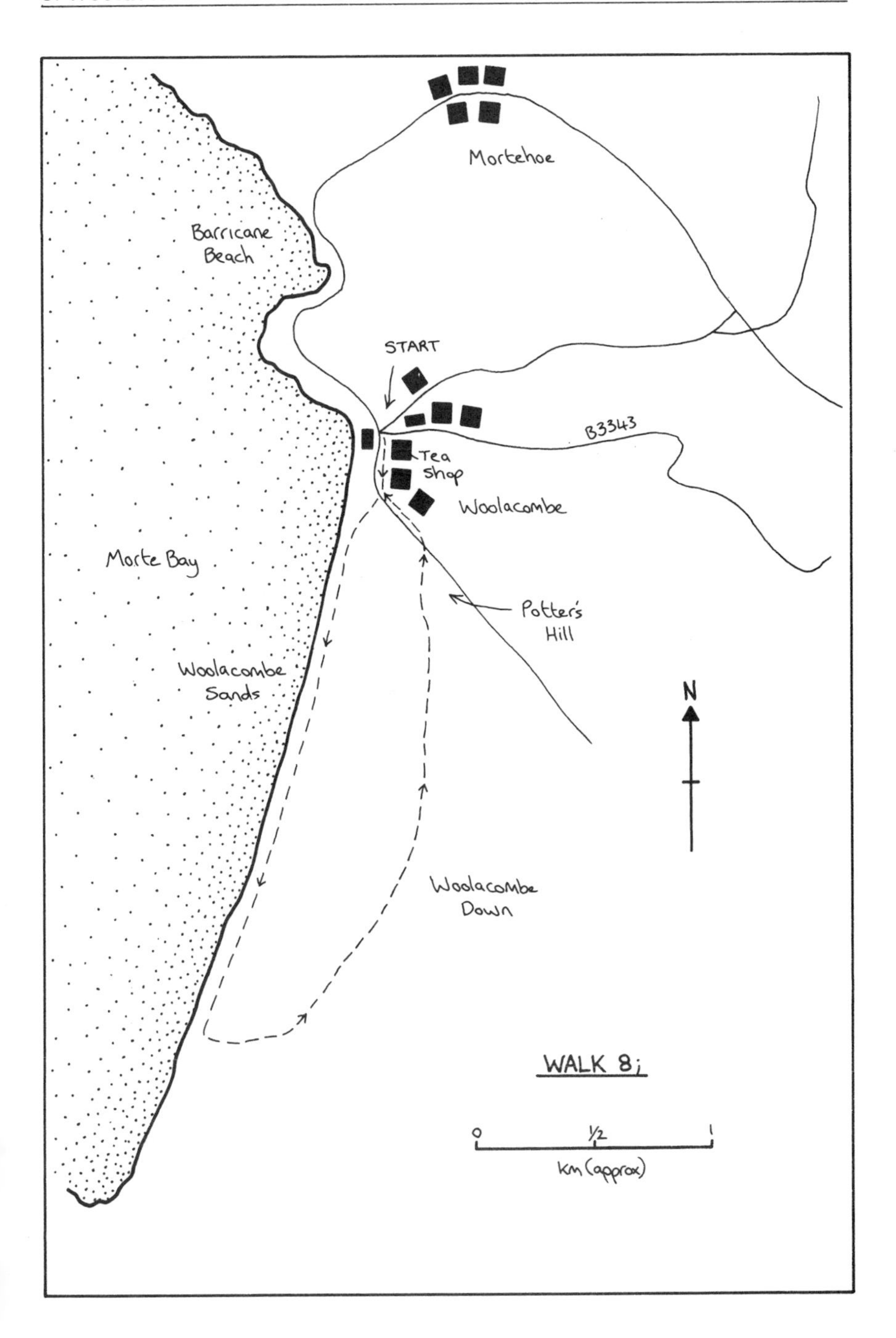
Mortehoe
Barricane Beach
START
B3343
Tea shop
Woolacombe
Morte Bay
Potter's Hill
Woolacombe Sands
N
Woolacombe Down
WALK 8;
0
½
1
km (approx)

9. Mortehoe

Length: 6¼ miles (10km); shorter version 5 miles (8km)

Summary: An excellent circuit including a fine section of the South West Coast Path, a superb track along the Morte Point peninsula and a return on a cross country path. Very little road walking. As in the case of much of the coast path, distances can be deceptive and the considerable rise and fall results in a walk which is more strenuous than is indicated by the mileage. The shorter version uses the Bull Point lighthouse access roadway as a very acceptable return to Mortehoe.

Car Parking: Pay and display car park at the top end of Mortehoe village. Grid reference 459452.

Map: Ordnance Survey Landranger no. 180, Barnstaple and Ilfracombe, 1:50,000.

The Tea Shop

At the point where the road starts to descend to Woolacombe and just past Mortehoe church is The Buttery on the left. It is a super restaurant – rather "arty" decor – dark green walls, lots of plants, even a fish tank – all very soothing and lots to look at whilst waiting for sustenance. The breakfast menu – served until noon, includes bumper bacon or sausage sandwiches, boiled eggs with toast "soldiers", and croissants. There is an extensive list of cooked meals available throughout the day. In the afternoon choose from Devonshire cream tea, or super Devonshire cream tea served with strawberries, "the hiker's tea" (very appropriate for this book!), or "New Orleans tea" – this includes pancakes with maple syrup or lemon and sugar. There is an interesting children's menu too. Certainly The Buttery is a place to linger and relax following the walk – highly recommended.

Open: 9.30am until at least 7.30pm every day in summer holiday months and open all the year. However, days and times can vary out-

The South West Coastal Path

side the main holiday season and it is advisable to telephone first. Tel: 01271 870610

About the area

Less of an out and out holiday resort than its neighbour Woolacombe, Mortehoe is an attractive old village perched high above Morte Bay. It is connected to Woolacombe by a steep and narrow little road which passes behind the famous sea shell Barricane Beach on the way. The village has several inns, restaurants and shops.

St Mary's parish church is mostly 14th century, including the tower, with a 13th century chancel and simple Norman north and south doorways. There are beautiful carved bench ends. The Mortehoe Heritage Centre, with a wealth of local material, adjoins the car park. It is open daily during high season, apart from Saturdays. In April, May, June and October it is closed on both Fridays and Saturdays.

Morte Point juts menacingly out to sea, as many vessels have found to their cost over the centuries. Near the end of the Point is a remarkable 'stickleback' spine of exposed rock. As National Trust owned land, there is unrestricted access. Further round the coast, Bull Point has a lighthouse. Lee and its valley are described in Walk no. 10.

The Walk

Turn left from the car park to walk through the village. Turn right to pass between the 'Ship Aground' Inn and the church, passing the public conveniences. Stay with the lane as far as the cemetery, where it loses its surface. Enter Morte Point Memorial Park at a kissing gate.

A delightful broad, grassy, track now heads for the Point. At any fork keep on towards the visible rocky spine, which lies just above the Point itself. The extensive views include Morte Bay, Woolacombe Sands and Baggy Point. Drifts of thrift contrast well with the acid yellow of the gorse.

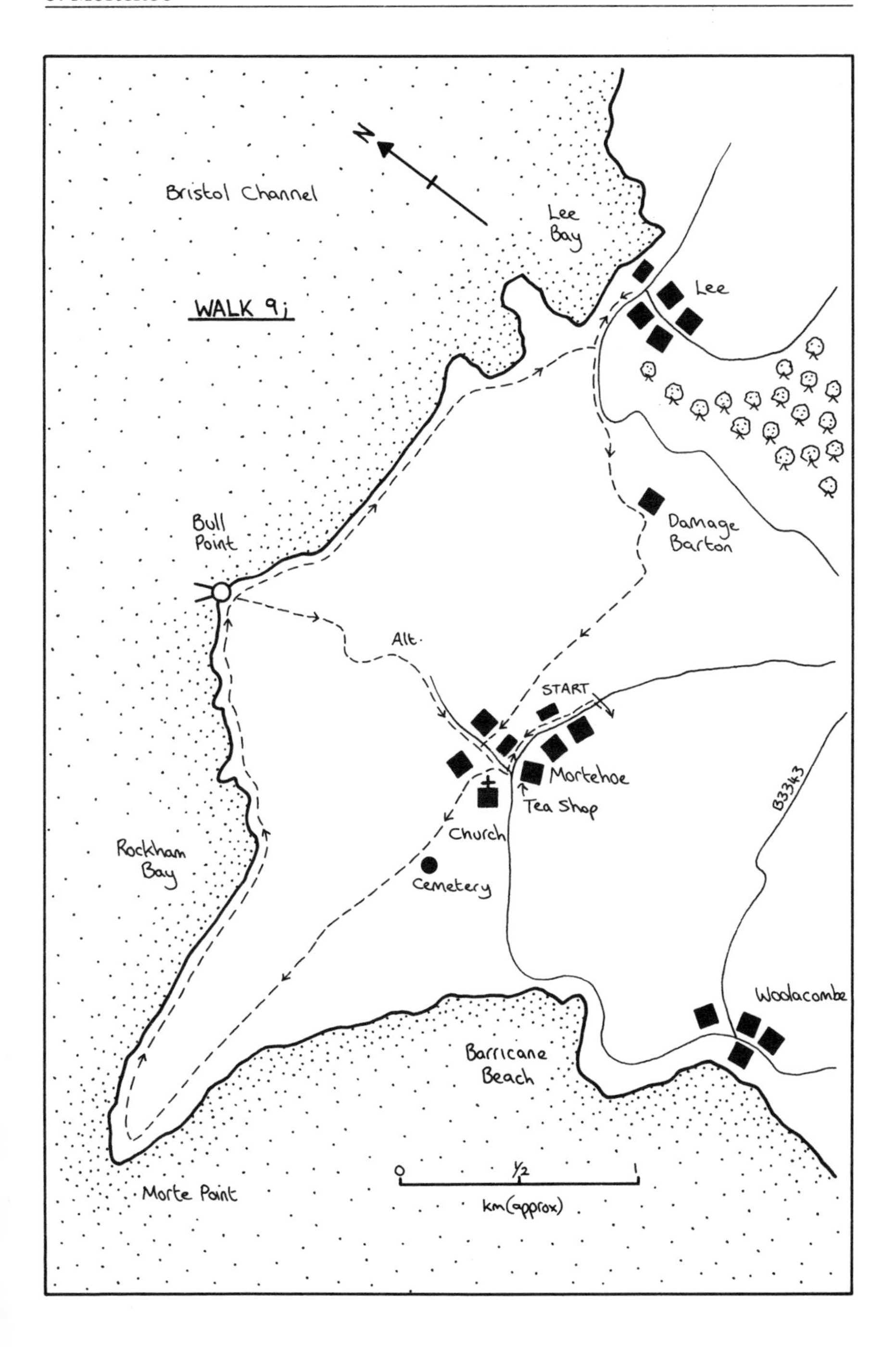
Bristol Channel
Lee Bay
Lee
WALK 9i
Damage Barton
Bull Point
Alt.
START
Mortehoe
Tea Shop
Church
Cemetery
B3343
Rockham Bay
Woolacombe
Barricane Beach
Morte Point
0
½
1
km (approx)

Join the coast path by the Point and turn right to head for Bull Point, with its prominent lighthouse. The fine rocky coastal scenery includes Rockham Bay. No route finding is necessary along this well-used path. There is one short exposed section – care with young children! Ignore any connecting paths and follow any 'coast path' sign.

For the shorter walk turn right at the lighthouse to return to Mortehoe along its access road.

For the full walk continue by the lighthouse perimeter fence to a yellow arrow and proceed towards Lee, the path being much as before. Reach a very minor road and descend towards Lee *(If you don't want to visit Lee you can save some distance and a steep ascent by turning right at the road)*

From Lee return up the same road, virtually traffic-free, rising straight from the cove, quite a long climb. As the road bends left, go straight on along an inviting track with a 'footpath' signpost, initially between high hedges. Go over a stile into an open meadow to join another track, bearing left by the side of a fence.

At a three-way signpost turn left towards Damage Barton. To the right is an obtrusive camping and caravan site. Pass the lovely old farmhouse and rise along the access drive. As the drive bends left, go over a waymarked stile/gate on the right to take an apparently little used path along the bottom of a field to another stile/gate. Pass Easewell Farm, with some ruined buildings.

Go right at a signposted stile/gate opposite the farm, pass a tiny pond and take the signposted route through the buildings of a large camping/caravan site. Follow a signpost to go straight ahead along a caravan site driveway. Exit through a gate to a road, close to the start of the Bull Point roadway, and turn left to return to Mortehoe.

10. Lee and Lower Slade

Length: 4¼ miles (6.8km)

Summary: The circuit combines coast path with a section of the former Ilfracombe branch railway line and field paths. Long ascent from Lee. Some public road along 'Fuschia Valley' to Lee. No difficulty underfoot although not all field paths are entirely evident on the ground.

Car Parking: Pay and display car park just behind the beach at Lee. Grid reference 480465.

Map: Ordnance Survey Outdoor Leisure no. 9, Exmoor, 1:25,000 (part of route only) or Landranger no. 190, Barnstaple and Ilfracombe, 1:50,000.

The Tea Shop

The valley leading down to the shore in Lee is called Fuchsia Valley – the venue for tea is the Fuchsia Tea Rooms and Tea Garden. This is a most pleasant place to enjoy morning coffee, a light lunch, or afternoon tea. The two tea rooms are small with pleasing decor – even the curtain fabric is patterned with fuchsias, as is the frieze round the walls.

Home-made soup is available each day. Also available are salads and a pasta bake. For something different there is "Hunters' Pie" made with ham and turkey and topped with cranberries. There is the usual but always welcome choice of goodies for tea, including home-made cakes, fruit loaf, scones, and sandwiches (including crab, when available). Beer and wines can be served with meals.

Open: every day, 10am – 5pm from Easter to the end of autumn half term holiday. Tel: 01271 863551

About the area

Lee is a pretty little place, straggling along the bottom of a thickly wooded valley which reaches well inland from the rocky bay and shingle beach. The mild climate encourages abundant growth of fuschias and other frost-hating plants, hence the 'fuschia valley' nickname. The village has hotel, inn with post office, tea shop and some thatched cottages.

Lower Slade is too close to Ilfracombe to have any particular individuality.

The 15-mile-long branch line of the former London and South Western Railway (later the Southern Railway), partially featured in this walk, was opened in July 1874, connecting the fast growing sea side resort of Ilfracombe with the already established railways at Barnstaple. It was a difficult branch, taking four years to construct. The high ground at Mortehoe necessitated a three mile climb at a gradient of 1 in 40 from the south and a particularly notorious climb of two miles at 1 in 36 on the return from Ilfracombe. Despite being obviously difficult to work, for many years it was a busy line; in 1909 there were 17 passenger trains each way on weekdays. Post World War II part of the prestigious 'Atlantic Coast Express' terminated at

Lee Bay

Ilfracombe and even Bulleid's 'West Country' pacific locomotives required extra help with trains of quite modest weight over this line.

Since closure in October 1970, much of the trackbed, including the part in this walk, has been developed as a cycleway and walking route.

The Walk

From the car park in Lee, walk towards the sea, turn right and pass the end of the Lee Bay Hotel. In 100m turn left at a ' coast path' signpost to follow a surfaced road uphill between hedge banks, permitting only occasional views of the wooded valley and the cove.

Pass a few outlying properties, still rising, with plenty of the fuschias for which Lee is famous in evidence. Go straight on at a signposted junction. After passing the last properties and a gate the road becomes 'unsuitable for motors', a grassy track now rising gently towards 'National Trust – Flat Point'.

Initially, the best long views are behind. Once over the gorse clad top, the surprise view is of The Torrs and Ilfracombe. Descend towards Ilfracombe; then bend right to a gate which gives access to Langleigh Lane, a straightforward downhill route to Lower Slade. Keep straight on as the lane becomes surfaced.

At the bottom of the lane turn right, then in 25m turn left into an unsurfaced road. In 100m bear right along a signposted bridleway leading directly to Lower Slade. Cross the road just above Lower Slade post office, bearing left to a 'public footpath' sign. Go up a broad track between houses. The track narrows as it passes along the back of more properties, rising to meet the former railway line. Go under the bridge and turn back, left, on to the trackbed.

Head away from Ilfracombe, keeping to the former line, restored as a cycling and walking route, for nearly two miles to the termination of the restored section by the B3231 road. Leave the line, turn left, and walk along the minor road towards Lee for 350m.

Turn left at the drive to Middle Campscott Farm ('public footpath' sign). Turn right at once over a waymarked stile and go along the edge of a meadow close to a fence on the right. Continue through a waymarked farm gate and keep the same line to another gate. Keep

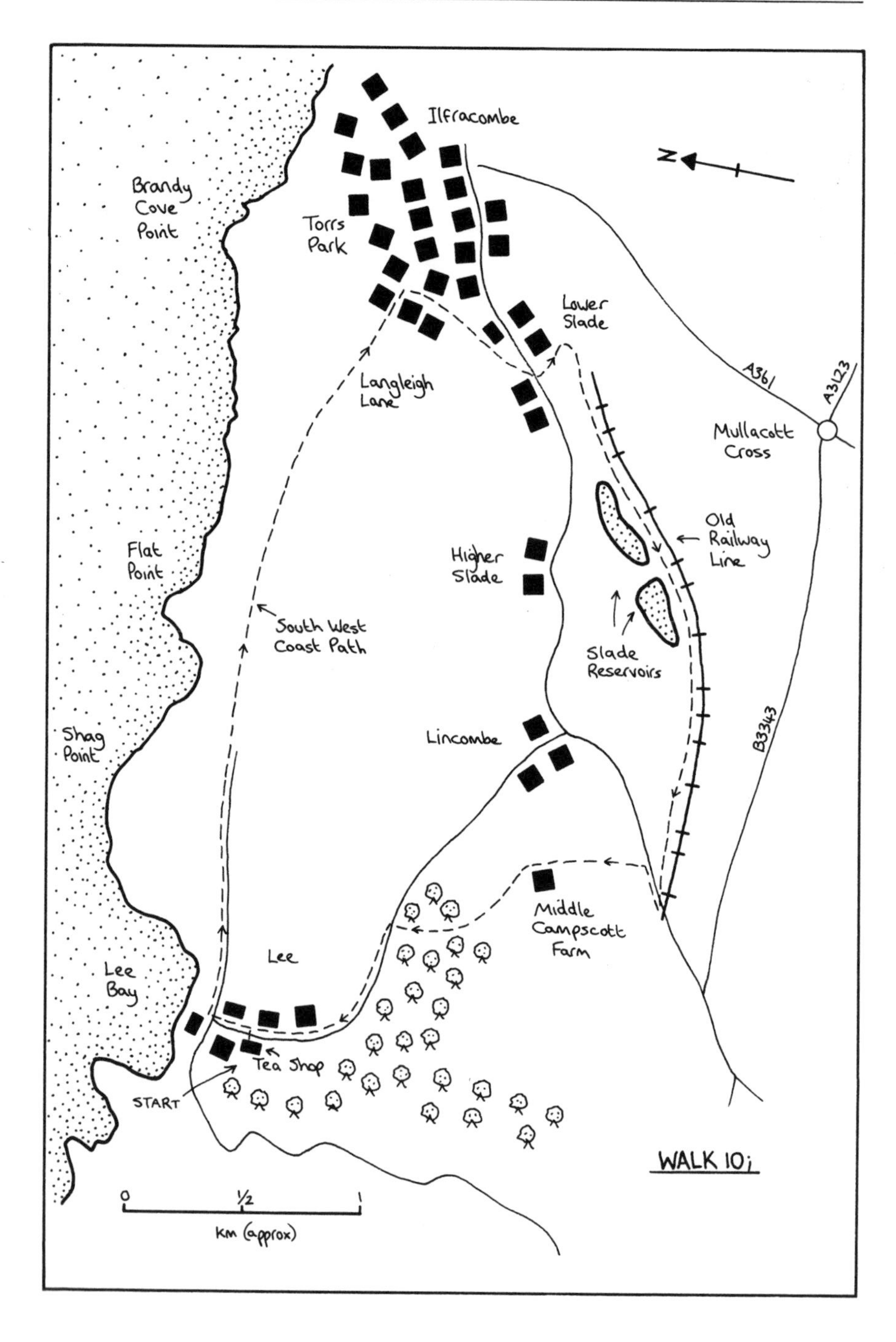
Ilfracombe
Brandy Cove Point
Torrs Park
Lower Slade
Langleigh Lane
A361
A3123
Mullacott Cross
Old Railway Line
Higher Slade
Flat Point
South West Coast Path
Slade Reservoirs
Shag Point
Lincombe
B3343
Middle Campscott Farm
Lee
Lee Bay
Tea Shop
START
WALK 10
0
½
1
km (approx)

straight on along a broad farm track, reaching the farm access drive close to the buildings.

Turn left down to the farm, then right between buildings to a gate and on to a second gate. Turn left after this gate, crossing a meadow which is without a worn path, slightly downhill, to a stile in the far boundary. There is a tiny stream on the left. Go over the stile and descend gently through a plantation of young trees, now on a marked path, to a gate leading into mature woodland.

The track is now broad as it continues the descent by the side of the stream. Go through a gate, cross a stream, and rise to the right to join a road. Turn left to walk down to Lee. The tea shop, just beyond the church, is unmissable.

11. Ilfracombe

Length: 4 miles (6.4km)

Summary: A remarkable walk combining some very fine coast path scenery with the bustling centre of Ilfracombe. A fair amount of rise and fall but with good paths and surfaced roadways underfoot.

Car Parking: Roadside parking by the entrance to Bicclescombe Park. Grid reference 517465.

Map: Ordnance Survey Outdoor Leisure no. 7, Exmoor, 1:25,000 or Landranger no. 180, Barnstaple and Ilfracombe area, 1:50,000.

The Tea Shop

Swiss Cottage Café is the chosen venue in the town centre. This is a typical English High Street café, owned and managed by a family, where the locals meet for coffee, lunch, or tea. It is, of course, also frequented by visitors to this popular resort who want to sample a cream tea or a high tea. However, this very English atmosphere is curiously combined with Swiss decor. The café is welcoming; service is pleasant even on a busy day. The waitresses all wear black dresses with long white aprons; the table linen is red and white gingham and the Swiss flag is much in evidence. Extensive all day menu and a separate children's menu. Open: 9am – 5pm everyday throughout the year but closed on Sundays. Tel: 01271 864433.

If a less bustling atmosphere is preferred, the walk may be continued to Biddlescombe Park before stopping for refreshment. The Old Mill, beautifully restored, is now an attractive tea room in a peaceful setting – it certainly deserves custom. Outside tables are also available. The menu includes light meals, cream teas, ice creams, tea, coffee, etc.

Open: June, July and August from 10.30am – 4pm every day. During the remainder of the season opening hours are very variable; it may be a good idea to check by 'phone if depending on this facility other than in the main holiday period. Closed in the winter months. Tel: 01271 862834.

About the area

Like many coastal holiday towns, Ilfracombe had a period of steady growth following the arrival of the railway in the second half of the 19th century. Again, like similar towns, there has been a post World War II decline, leaving much of the town rather tacky and down at heel. Fortunately, considerable efforts are being made to revitalise a large and important part of the town centre. There is a good harbour which, in the great days, was vibrant with crowds of passengers enjoying the numerous steamer excursions. Now, there are occasional sailings to and from Lundy.

Long before the tourists arrived, Ilfracombe was an ancient port with a market charter of 1278. Standing above the harbour, St Nicholas Chapel on Lantern Hill was built about 1300 and dedicated

Coast path near Ilfracombe

to the patron saint of seamen. In later years it also served as a lighthouse. Renovation was carried out in 1962 and the chapel is open to visitors. The town's other really old building is Holy Trinity church, an enlargement of a Norman church on the site of a Saxon church. The wagon roof is particularly good.

As would be expected in a town of this size, there are comprehensive shopping and refreshment facilities. Of interest to visitors are the tunnel beaches, with the original bath house nearby, and Ilfracombe Museum, with a considerable collection of artefacts and pictures, praised by the late John Betjeman. The tunnel bored under the seaward ridge of high ground reaches otherwise inaccessible beaches and the museum is housed in the former laundry building of the old Ilfracombe Hotel, in the pleasure gardens.

The setting of the town is superb, Hillsborough and the Torrs standing guard to east and west respectively, with more gradually rising high ground inland. A ridge of high ground and Capstone Hill separate the body of the town from the sea.

Bicclescombe Park is a pleasant open space with well-kept grounds, including tennis courts and a restored water mill, part of which is used as a tea room. The Torrs area or 'Seven Hills' is fine coastal upland, owned by the National Trust. The coast path which zig zags down from the summit above jagged rocks is spectacular and has been very well engineered.

The Walk

Pass the restored water mill and walk through the park between ponds and tennis courts, aiming for a gate at the far right corner. Cross the road to Park Way opposite and rise to the right along a roughish track to the main road.

Cross with care and continue up Kingsley Avenue, soon levelling out and continuing as a rather rough road. The Cairn Nature Reserve is above to the left. Go straight on, slightly downhill; note the 'Round House' above to the left. Pass the site of the former railway terminus, under development in 1997, with the Pall factory, environmentally acclaimed, to the left.

Go ahead, downhill, along Station Road. Turn left into Richmond

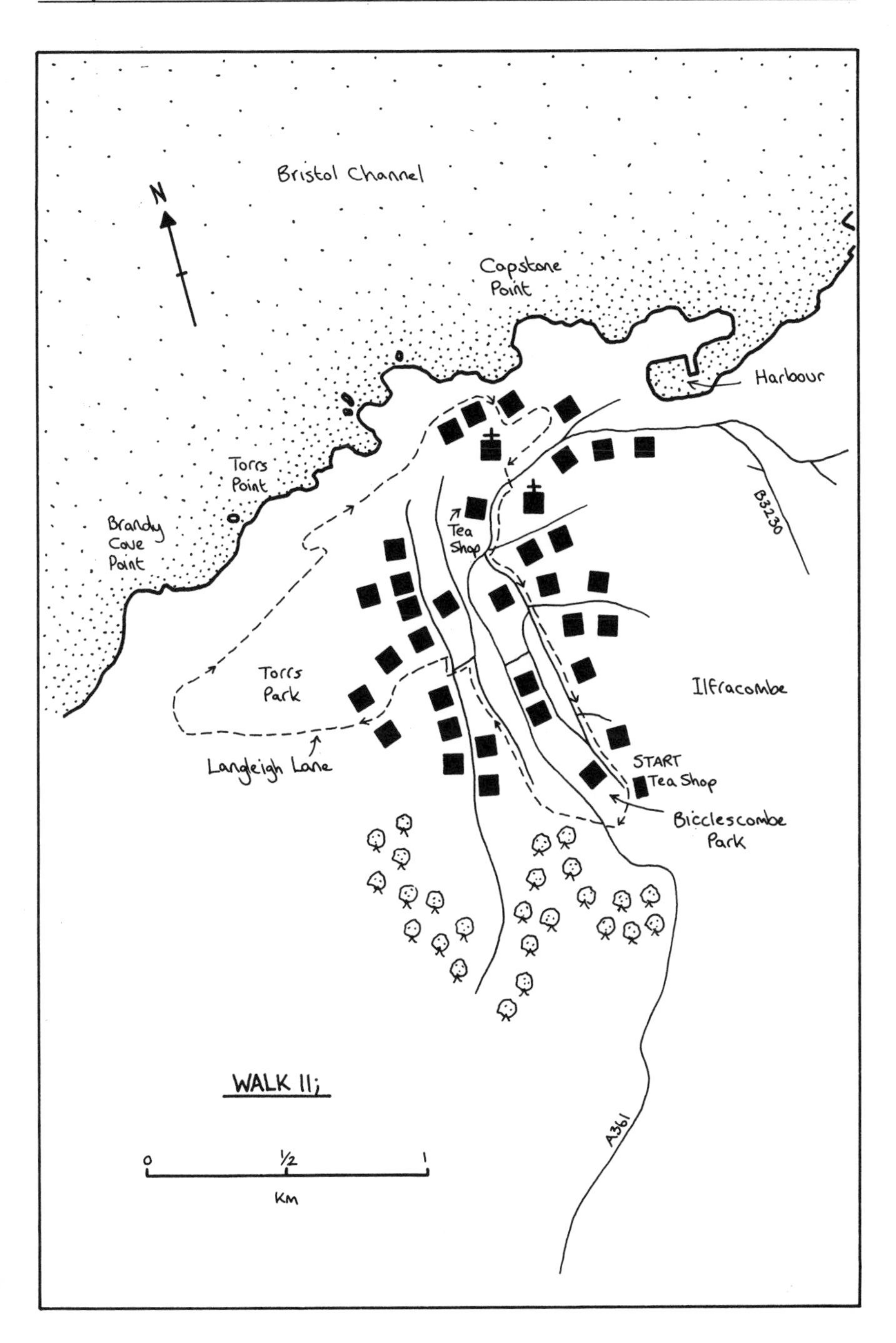
Bristol Channel
N
Capstone Point
Harbour
Torrs Point
Brandy Cove Point
B3230
Tea Shop
Torrs Park
Ilfracombe
Langleigh Lane
START
Tea Shop
Bicclescombe Park
WALK 11;
A361
0
½
1
Km

Road. At the junction at the end turn right and, in less than 50m, turn left into Broad Park Avenue. Hereabouts there are good examples of typical turn of the century seaside houses with balconies. Cross a tiny stream and, as the road begins to rise, turn left into Langleigh Park, leading to Langleigh Lane.

In 50m turn right into Langleigh Lane to commence a long ascent, initially on tarmac. Go straight on as the tarmac bends to the right. The unsurfaced lane is now a typical old Devon thoroughfare, with the hedgerows bright with red campion, wild briar and many others. A communications mast is visible to the left. At the top of the lane go through a gate with a 'National Trust, Langleigh Valley' sign and bear right to a stile.

Continue along the South West Coast Path, winding around the fine Torrs area, with wonderful sea views. Away to the left is Bull Point with its lighthouse (see the Mortehoe walk). A summit ahead may be ascended by using a stile or by-passed to the right. If by-passed, go through a farm gate, then left and right, angling uphill on a track which is initially surfaced, with a gorse hedge to the left. There is now a bird's eye view of Ilfracombe, with Hillsborough beyond.

Go up to a gate and turn right, soon commencing the descent of an amazing series of zig zags poised hundreds of feet above the sea. Go up a few steps to enter residential Ilfracombe. Turn left at a coast path sign to follow Torrs Walk Avenue, an unsurfaced residential road. At a junction go ahead along Granville Road. Wildersmouth Beach is below and Capstone Hill stands out in front.

As the road bends sharp right, go through a little gate on the left and descend through a small park, past the museum, to Wilder Road. There is a pretty bandstand in Runnymede Gardens, to the right. At Wilder Road turn left towards the Tourist Information Centre and then up to the right towards the library and the Citizens Advice Bureau.

Here, on the right, is the start of 'the lanes', essentially a series of rear access alleyways, decorated with mosaic murals and wrought iron, depicting local scenes. At the far end is Market Square. Turn left, under the arches, where there are fine bronze murals of Ilfracombe past and present.

At the busy High Street turn right, soon reaching the selected tea shop. Continue along High Street, then Church Street, to the junction with Horne Road. Turn left and go uphill to a junction with a ramped right turn. At the next junction fork left into Furze Hill Road. The modest elevation gives views over much of Ilfracombe, to the Pall factory and the Torrs beyond.

As the road bends left, uphill, go straight ahead into a tarmac track signposted 'footpath to Bicclescombe Park', leading directly to the park and the parking area.

12. Hele and Berrynarbour

Length: 5¾ miles (9.2km)

Summary: A very rewarding walk of immense variety, including fine coastal scenery, rather more demanding than the mileage indicates. From Berrynarbour there is an ascent to cross the hill top at 578ft (176m), whilst the return from Hele has an initial climb followed by the meandering coast path with plenty of rise and fall. Interesting features include a restored water powered mill, one of England's oldest manor houses and a nineteenth century castle which is now equipped as a visitor attraction. Generally good underfoot but some mud likely.

Car Parkng: In Berrynarbour village, 50m up the hill, just beyond the church. Grid reference 562466. For an alternative start at Hele, there is a large free car park. Grid reference 535478.

Map: Ordnance Survey Outdoor Leisure no. 9, Exmoor, 1:25,000 or Landranger no. 180, Barnstaple and Ilfracombe, 1:50,000.

The Tea Shop

The chosen place for refreshment is The Tea Room and Garden at Chambercombe Manor. However, it has not been possible to sample this venue as, at the time of writing, it was closed for improvements and alterations. By the publication date it will have re-opened and should prove to be very pleasant for morning coffee, lunch, or afternoon tea. Chambercombe Manor is interesting to look round but the tea room can be accessed quite independently.

Open: 10.30am – 5pm Monday – Friday and from 2.30pm – 5pm on Sundays from Easter Sunday until the end of September Closed on Saturdays. Tel: 01271 862624

As an alternative, just a little further along the route of the walk, refreshments and cream teas can be obtained at Hele Mill. There are only two tables in the very small shop but plenty of seating in the mill garden.

About the area

Berrynarbour is a pleasant place situated on one side of the Sterridge valley, close to popular holiday resorts yet sufficiently off the beaten track to remain as a quiet, unspoilt, Devon village, with inn and post office. The church has an impressive 15th century tower and a massive Norman font.

The warm, sheltered, Sterridge valley has a distinct feel of South rather than North Devon. Flowers from the cottage gardens spill over, mingling with the abundant wild flowers of the roadside.

A rather nondescript outlying part of Ilfracombe, Hele has its own small rocky bay. Most interesting is the water-powered corn mill, claimed to be originally of 1525, now restored from dereliction and able to produce stone ground flour and other cereals. On the same site is a small pottery and a tea garden. In a sheltered valley

Chambercombe Manor

bottom close to Hele is Chambercombe Manor, a very old property indeed, with 16th and 17th century buildings and fine old furniture, open to the public during the season. The recommended tea room is in part of the Manor.

Watermouth Castle is a 19th century mansion, now equipped as a comprehensive visitor and amusement centre, with collections of bygones and plenty of interest for children. Below the Castle is a fine harbour, indented in the rocky coastline in a way unusual in North Devon.

The Walk

From the car park in Berrynarbour go past the church and turn left to follow a road signposted 'Sterridge Valley'. Pass the post office and descend steeply to the bottom of the Sterridge valley, turning left to follow the delightful little road for about three quarters of a mile.

As the road bends left, turn right to take a signposted 'public footpath Trayne'. Go through a gate and rise steeply up the valley side. Keep to the upper edge of two fields, passing a post with waymark. Cross a tiny stream on a wooden bridge and pass through an area carpeted with ransoms (wild garlic). Reach a huge meadow at a stile and carry on towards a signpost visible by a stile at the top boundary.

The next field may well be found to be cultivated; however, the line of the right of way is as indicated by the signpost, bearing a little to the right to another signpost and stile giving access to a minor road. Some walkers may prefer to keep to the edge of this field, in which case follow the hedge to the left.

Cross the road and take the farm driveway descending to Lower Trayne, with splendid views to the Hele area of Ilfracombe. Go through the farm; after the exit gate keep left on a clear track descending past a marker post into the attractive Hele valley.

Go through a gate, cross a stream and continue along a possibly muddy track to Comyn farmyard. Go straight through the yard and follow an old sign to 'Ilfracombe'. The lane leads directly to Chambercombe Manor, with tea room. After leaving the Manor, continue to a residential area, turning right to walk down Chambercombe

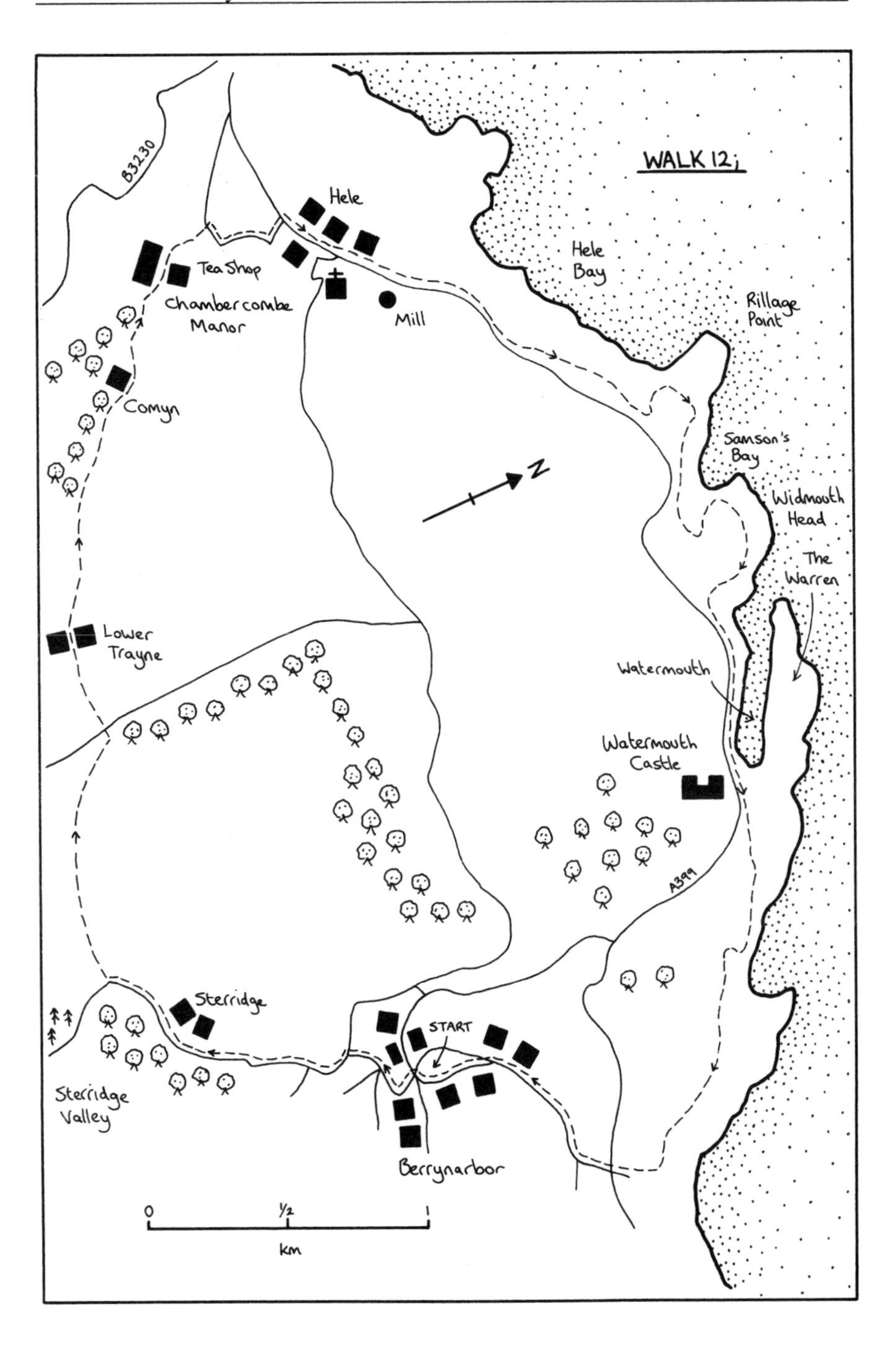
WALK 12
B3230
Hele
Tea Shop
Chambercombe Manor
Mill
Hele Bay
Rillage Point
Comyn
Samson's Bay
N
Widmouth Head
The Warren
Lower Trayne
Watermouth
Watermouth Castle
A399
Sterridge
START
Sterridge Valley
Berrynarbor
0
1/2
1
km

Park Road to the main A399 road. Turn right to descend to Hele, with Hele Mill well signposted on the right.

With or without a short diversion to Hele Bay, walk uphill beside the main road; the savage coastal cliffs hereabouts leave no space for a path between road and sea. Forty metres before the entrance to Ilfracombe golf club turn left at a 'coast path' signpost and stay with this path, turning left down steps at an informal car park. The coastal scenery back towards Ilfracombe is among the finest in Devon, with the great mound of Hillsborough dominant.

The path weaves in and out and up and down quite strenuously as it passes behind Rillage Point and Samson's Bay. There is good waymarking and signposting and the route is never in doubt. Widmouth Head is passed by long flights of steps, up and down, and the path then enters woodland thick with bluebells along the side of Water Mouth, with its little harbour at the head of the cove.

Soon there is a choice – a high tide route or a low tide route. The former is along the side of the adjacent road for a short distance, whilst the latter skirts the edge of the harbour. The roadside route has views of Watermouth Castle. After rejoining, the way becomes a rather overgrown track close to the roadside.

Return briefly to the road, cross a stream and turn left at a 'coast path' sign, rising along the edge of a touring caravan site to a ladder stile. Turn left here along the unsurfaced Old Coast Road. Go straight across a surfaced road by the entrance to the Sandy Cove Hotel and take a cul de sac road rising to the main road. Go across into Barton Lane at a 'Berrynarbour ½ mile' sign to amble back, mainly downhill, into the village.

13. Combe Martin and Great Hangman

Length: 5 miles (8km)

Summary: A fine circuit using the South West Coast Path to climb from Combe Martin to the 1044ft (318m) summit of Great Hangman, with an excellent return route. As the start is close to sea level, this is the greatest ascent in the book. However, the gradients are not excessive and there are no difficulties underfoot.

Car Parking: Pay and Display car park with public conveniences close to the harbour in Combe Martin. Grid reference 578473.

Map: Ordnance Survey Outdoor Leisure no. 9, Exmoor, 1:25,000 or Landranger no. 180, Barnstaple and Ilfracombe, 1:50,000.

The Tea Shop

It was not easy to choose a tea shop in Combe Martin but eventually we decided upon The Redwood Eating House. This is truly a seaside café! It overlooks a small shingle beach and the sea. The café is part of a seaside gift and postcard shop. Decor is smart and clean. Tables have marble tops and the crockery is attractive. Counter service system in operation with an immense menu at very reasonable prices. Thoroughly recommended is the buttered apricot tea bread. Open: 9.30am – 6pm every day from mid-March to end of October. Tel: 01271 883407

About the area

Combe Martin is an unusual place. Situated in a deep valley, tightly squeezed between high ground on each side, significant expansion of the village has necessitated building ever further inland from the rocky harbour where facilities are concentrated. The result is a continuously built-up main street no less than two miles in length with no side streets of any consequence.

Close to Combe Martin silver and lead mines were worked for several centuries, finally ceasing production as recently as 1875. There are very few visible remains of this once important industry.

The parish church is towards the inland end of the village, very fine indeed, with a large 15th century tower, 13th century chancel, wooden chancel screen and old animal carvings on the benches.

More curious is the 18th century Pack O' Cards Inn, now a listed building, constructed by a gambler who is said to have made a great deal of money from card playing. There are 52 windows, 13 rooms and 4 floors.

Close to the harbour is the Combe Martin Motorcycle Collection, whilst above the village at Higher Leigh Manor is a wildlife and leisure park.

The coastal hills between Combe Martin and Heddon's Mouth are among the highest in the West Country and the scenery is superb.

The Walk

Leave the car park at its upper end. Follow a sign 'Coast Path, Lester Point etc.' and pass the Exmoor National Park boundary marker to start the long rise to Little Hangman and Great Hangman.

Close to Lester Point the path turns sharp right then passes behind the difficult of access Wild Pear beach. Ahead the sharp point of Little Hangman crowns the gorse-clad slopes tumbling for hundreds of feet to the sea. Just short of the summit, by a seat, there is a choice – straight on over the top or by-passing the summit by turning right.

Great Hangman now dominates the view ahead, approached along a lovely grassy track, climbing inexorably. The top of Great Hangman is a wild, windswept place, capped by a great heap of stones, with a signpost embedded.

Continue along the coast path, bending to the right. To the left the next great mound is Holdstone Down, fractionally higher than Great

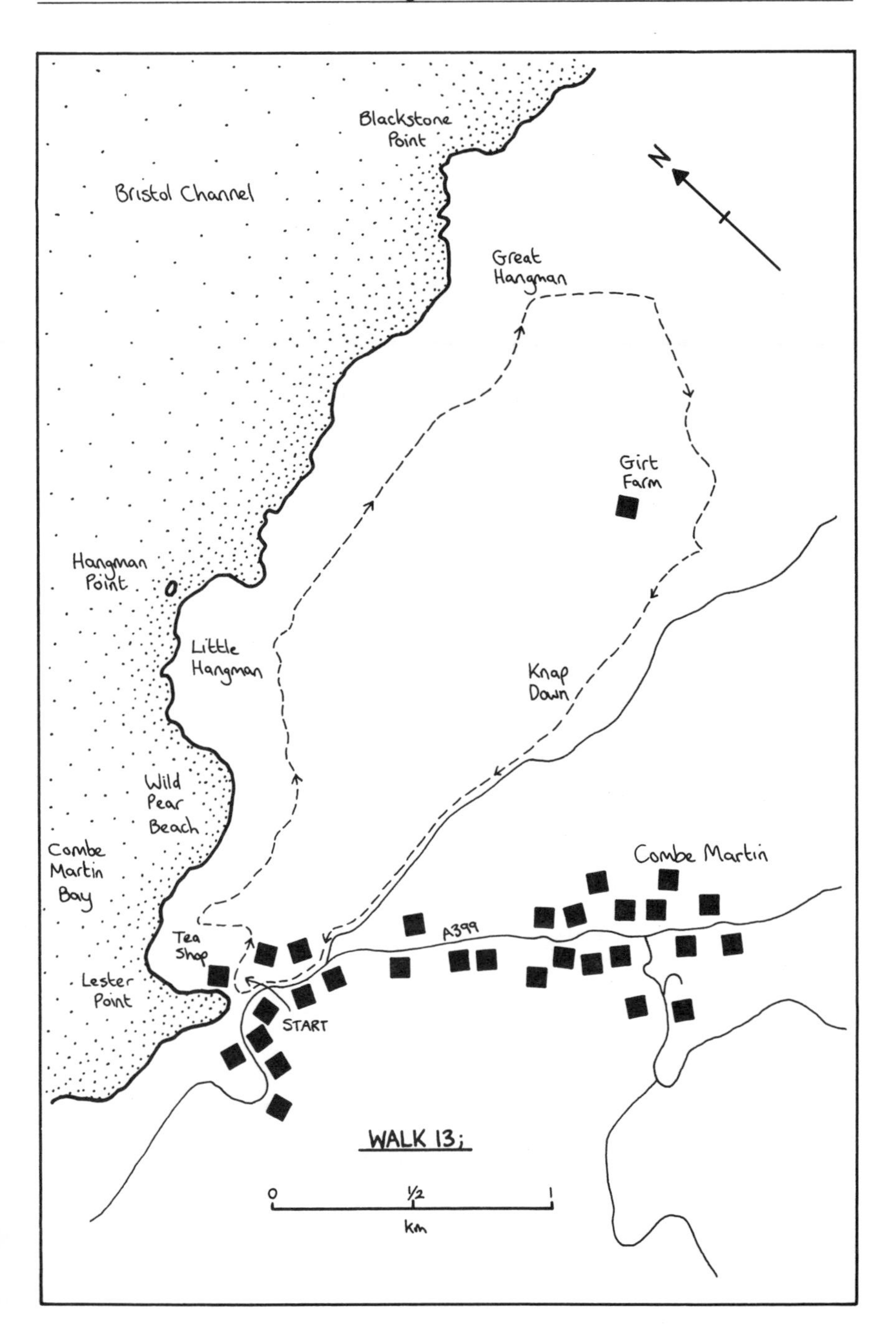
Blackstone Point
Bristol Channel
N
Great Hangman
Girt Farm
Hangman Point
Little Hangman
Knap Down
Wild Pear Beach
Combe Martin Bay
Combe Martin
Tea Shop
A399
Lester Point
START
WALK 13;
0
½
1
km

Little Hangman

Hangman. At a signpost by the angle of a wall, turn right for 'Combe Martin and County Road' The path stays close to the wall on the left to reach a gate with a 'pass through sheep pens' notice Keep the wall close on the left and go through two gates at a sheep gathering area.

The route is now along a stony roadway, descending steadily. At the top of a rise turn right into a path signposted 'Combe Martin via Knap Down Lane'. Parts of this path may be a little muddy but it is otherwise first rate, with splendid views of Little Hangman and of Combe Martin Bay, below.

On reaching a minor road turn right, downhill. Stay with the road until it turns sharp left. At this point go straight ahead along a footpath which continues the same line of descent towards the sea end of the village street. At a junction of several routes go ahead to pass below the school. Turn right at the main street to reach the tea shop. The car park is just behind, past the Tourist Information Centre

14. Hunter's Inn and Trentishoe

Length: 3¾ miles (6km). Shorter version omitting Trentishoe is half a mile less.

Summary: A walk of modest length, but with a long steep ascent on tarmac. However, it is worth every foot of that climb to enjoy the exhilarating length of coast path perched 600ft (183m) above the sea and the bird's eye view of Heddon's Mouth. No problems underfoot apart from a little scree on the way down into the Heddon Valley. Children will need careful supervision on part of the coast path.

Car Parking: Field owned by National Trust and some adjacent roadside spaces at Hunter's Inn. Grid reference 655480.

Map: Ordnance Survey Outdoor Leisure no.9, Exmoor, 1;25,000 or Landranger no. 180, Barnstaple and Ilfracombe, 1;50,000.

Tea Shop

Hunter's Inn is the chosen venue; this well known hostelry is an absolute "mecca" for visitors to this part of Devon. Many walkers call here for coffee in the morning, bar lunches, and afternoon teas which are available from 3pm. Indeed as there are two rambles returning to this point, walkers may enjoy more than one visit! Open throughout the year. Tel: 01598 763230.

Description

Hunter's Inn is sufficiently well known to have the distinction of its name on the ordnance survey maps, even at 1:50,000 scale. The situation is remarkable, with three valleys coming together at this poimt. Trentishoe is a farming hamlet nestling in a protective fold in the high moorland. The small, plain, church has survived despite a steady decrease in the parish population from almost 100 to less

Peacock at Hunter's Inn

than 50 in the last 100 years or so. Close to the hamlet are the high dowland tops of Trentishoe Down and Holdstone Down, both readily visited from car parks along the side of the minor road which serves Trentishoe.

Inevitably, Hunter's Inn has become a very popular centre for visitors and the National Trust has provided a shop and information centre, public conveniences and extra car parking.

The Walk

Pass to the left of Hunter's Inn and follow the road past a terrace of cottages. Turn right immediately into a very minor road signposted 'Trentishoe Church - unfit for motors'. The climb starts at once.

To omit Trentishoe, turn right before the top of the climb to take a footpath on the right by an N.T. 'Trentishoe Combe' notice and an 'access to coast path' signpost.

After visiting Trentishoe, return down the road to the notice and

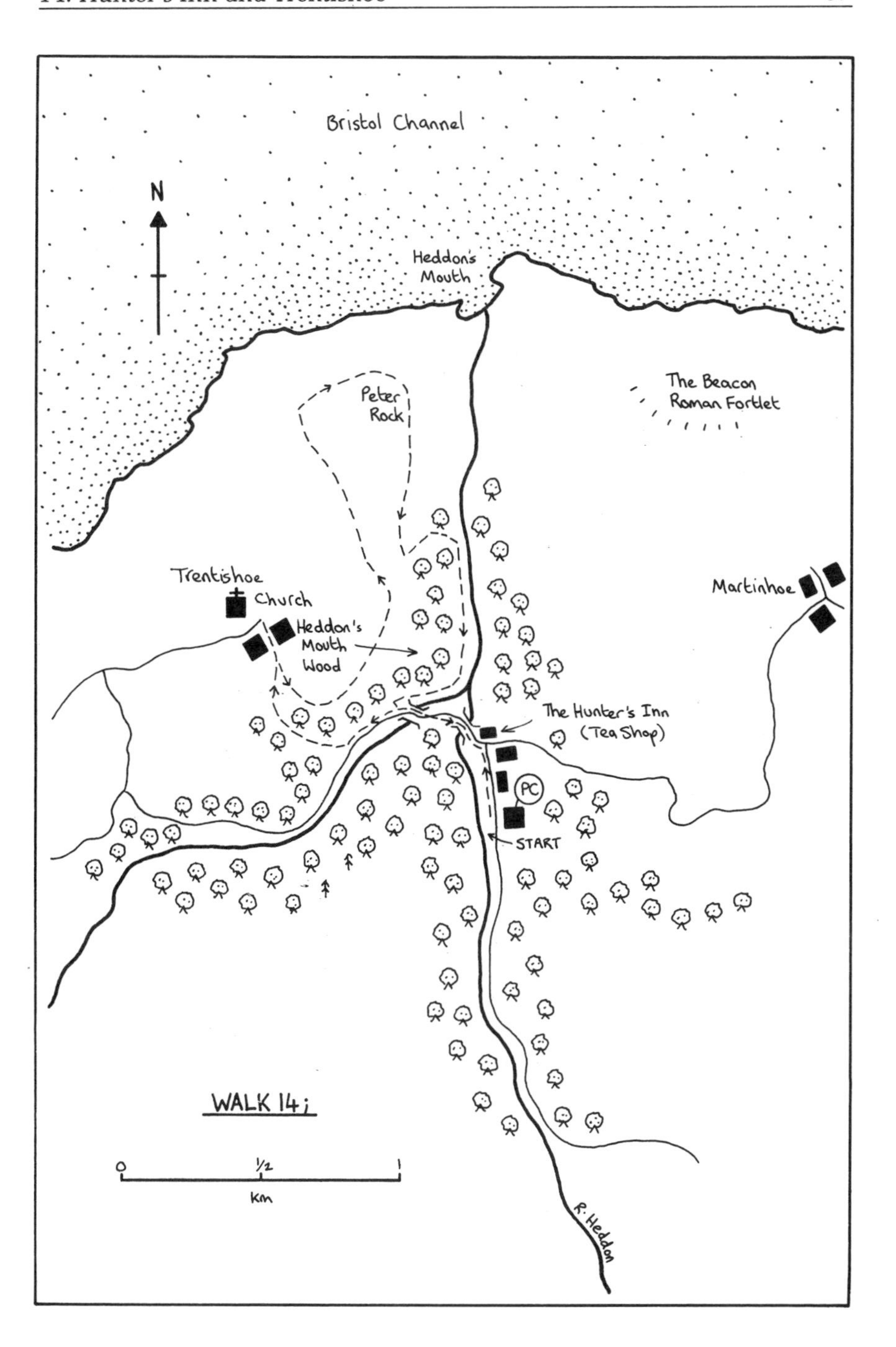
Bristol Channel
N
Heddon's Mouth
Peter Rock
The Beacon Roman Fortlet
Trentishoe Church
Heddon's Mouth Wood
Martinhoe
The Hunter's Inn (Tea Shop)
PC
START
WALK 14i
0
1/2
1
km
R. Heddon

sign as above and turn left. A grassy path rises, with a traditional Devon wall/bank on the left. There are good views over Hunter's Inn, the three valleys which meet at that point and a hotel on the valley side.

Bear left round the angle of a wall and across a neck of land to reveal sudden views for miles along the coast to the west, including Great Hangman and Little Hangman. Go slightly downhill to a three way sign. Turn right here to follow 'coast path', a delightful route across the steep hillside 600ft (183m) above the rolling swell of the sea, with the scenery enhanced by rocky outcrops.

The path bends right to contour above the Heddon Valley, the views now being of the cove and shingle beach at Heddon's Mouth and the valley generally. The descent starts with some rudimentary steps followed by scree, soon reaching the valley bottom woodland amidst myriads of bluebells in Spring. Join the main path from Heddon's Mouth and turn right to walk to the road. Turn left at the road to return to Hunter's Inn and the raucous screech of the peacocks which infest this area.

15. Hunter's Inn and Heddon's Mouth

Length: 2 miles (3.2km)

Summary: Short and easy, but one of the classic walks of North Devon, through a deep wooded valley to a rocky cove with shingle beach. No ascent, no route finding problems and entirely good underfoot.

Car Parking: Close to Hunter's Inn. Field owned by National Trust and some adjacent roadside spaces. Grid reference 655480.

Map: Ordnance Survey Outdoor Leisure no. 9, Exmoor, 1:25,000 or Landranger no. 180, Barnstaple and Ilfracombe, 1:50,000.

The Tea Shop

See Walk 14.

About the area

For Hunter's Inn, see walk 14. Three valleys join at the inn, from which point the River Heddon hustles through richly diverse woodland to reach the sea at Heddon's Mouth. Deep and lush, this is possibly the most attractive of North Devon's sea-going valleys, rich in plant and wild life, with the stark contrast of high, wind-swept, downs on either side. At Heddon's Mouth a lime kiln worked until the 19th century, coal from South Wales being landed at the cove and used in combination with the local limestone to produce lime for the fields and as a building material. A few years ago the kiln was carefully restored but unfortunately there has been subsequent damage making further restoration necessary.

The Walk

Walk along the road to Hunter's Inn and bear right; take a broad, easy, track on the left signposted 'Martinhoe, Woody Bay and Heddon's Mouth'. At a fork take the lesser path, on the left. Pass a modern looking stone bridge but don't cross it.

Keep left at the next fork, to 'Heddon's Mouth', close by the river, here rushing in its eagerness to reach the sea. Pass by another footbridge before reaching the back of the cove. Cross the river on stepping stones just before it disappears into the beach shingle, and climb the temporary steps below the old lime kiln. *Or, go back to the last foot bridge if preferred.*

Turn left to head back up the valley along another wide, easy, track. At a fork keep right, to a gate and continue to a minor road. Turn left to return to the car park and Hunter's Inn.

Heddon's Mouth

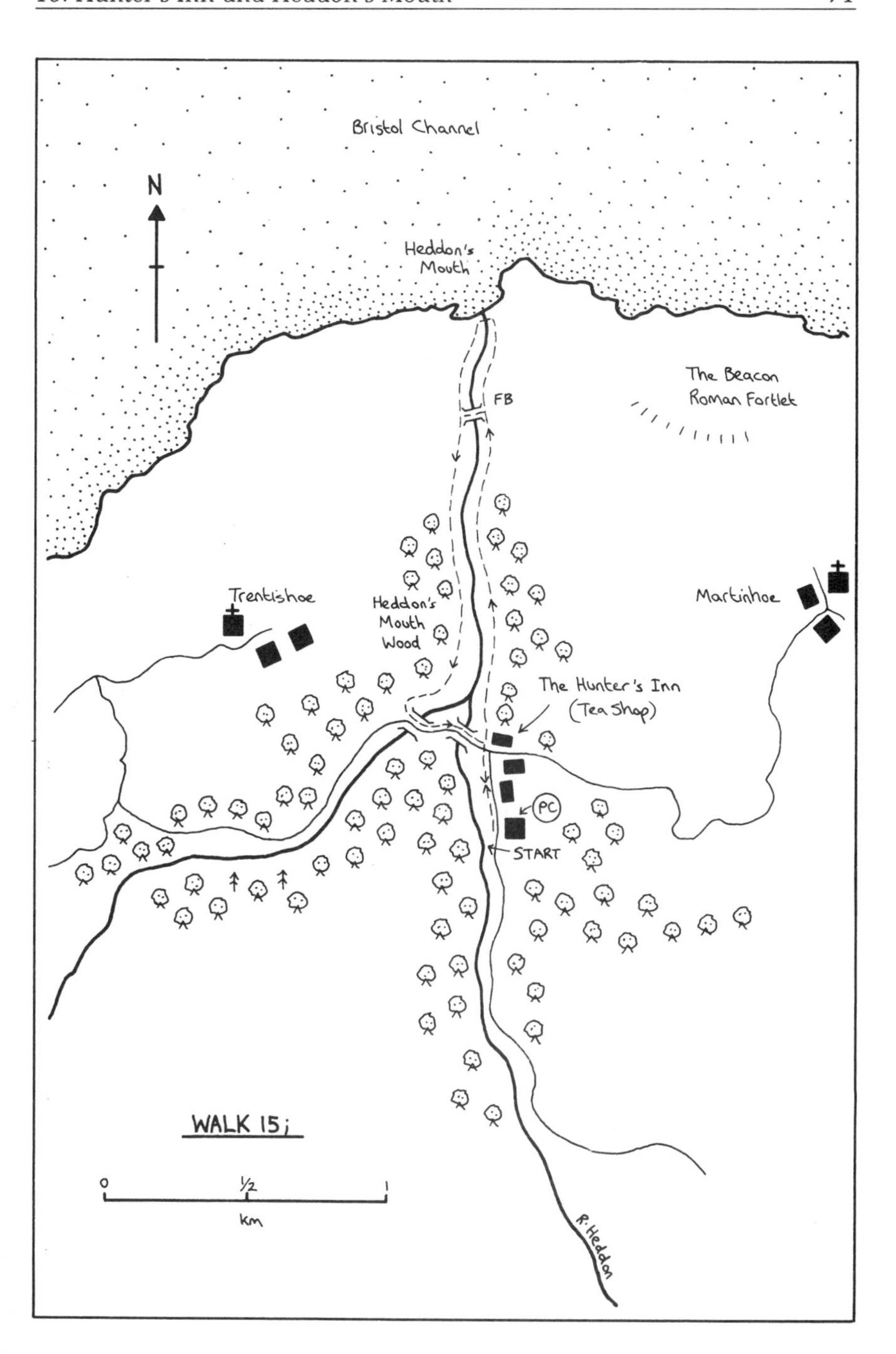
Bristol Channel
N
Heddon's Mouth
FB
The Beacon Roman Fortlet
Trentishoe
Heddon's Mouth Wood
Martinhoe
The Hunter's Inn (Tea Shop)
PC
START
WALK 15;
0
½
1
km
R. Heddon

16. Lynton and the Valley of the Rocks

Length: 4 miles (6.4km)

Summary: A circuit including the spectacular scenery of the Valley of the Rocks, both at close quarters and seen from the top of the moor to the south of the valley. Long ascent of the valley side – 170m (558ft). Very good underfoot, including a fair amount of tarmac.

Car Parking: Main pay and display car park with public conveniences in Lynton. Grid reference 721493.

Map: Ordnance Survey Outdoor Leisure no. 9, Exmoor, 1:25,000 or Landranger no. 180, Barnstaple and Ilfracombe area, 1:50,000.

The Tea Shop

The Tea Cottage is a venture operated by the Lay Community at Lee Abbey – a Christian conference and holiday centre of the Anglican Faith. Teas are served in the garden which is beautiful; it will certainly be of interest to amateur gardeners – here is a true cottage garden with old trees and old fashioned flowers such as Californian poppies, lupins, etc. and a buddleia to attract the butterflies. Understandably there is a limited menu – soup and sandwiches are served at lunch time whilst cream teas, cakes, ice creams, are available during the afternoon. The scones are excellent and one idea which other tea shops might advantageously add to their menu is the "small" cream tea – very reassuring for those contemplating a large evening meal.

Open: summer months only, 11am – 5pm daily but last orders at 4pm. Closed on Sundays and Mondays. Appropriate only in fine weather. Tel: 01598 752621 – Lee Abbey. Note: When this recommended venue is not functioning, teas etc. can be obtained in Lynton.

About the area

To most people Lynton and Lynmouth are indivisible. They are, however, two very different communities, close together in distance but separated by a steep hillside.

Lynmouth is a small seaside resort based on an old fishing village squeezed between sea and hillsides, whilst Lynton is a small and, it must be said, rather ordinary small town on high ground above. The difference in altitude is around 150m (500ft). The two are linked by a long-established cliff railway.

Lynmouth's major claim to fame is that the village was devastated by a great flood on 15th August, 1952, when the normally charming and much admired East and West Lyn rivers changed character with incredible suddenness, becoming raging torrents following prolonged heavy rain on Exmoor. The floodwater destroyed bridges, houses, shops and hotels. Cars and wreckage were carried out to sea and 34 lives were lost. Reconstruction, including measures designed to prevent any repetition, has been carried out with great care.

The privately owned Glen Lyn Gorge, with waterfalls and a collection of steam engine models, may be visited on payment. The gorge is designated as a Site of Special Scientific Interest. Also in Lynmouth is the Exmoor Brass Rubbing and Hobbycraft Centre, with free admission.

Apart from the church, with 13th century tower, and the old town hall, there are few buildings of interest in Lynton. The Moorland Museum in Market Street has a traditional Exmoor kitchen and maritime exhibits; also featured is the Lynton and Barnstaple Railway. In Queen Street is Miniature Autoworld, with a toy museum and shop.

Even on a coastline which has many miles of fine rocky scenery, the Valley of the Rocks is outstanding. A dry valley with rugged limestone formations known as tors, many having individual names such as Castle Rock, Rugged Jack and Chimney Rock, it may well have been the original route by which the Lyn River reached the sea. Coastal erosion, weathering by wind, rain and ice have all contributed to the diversion of the river and the present scenery. One doesn't need to be a geologist to appreciate that this valley really is different.

Beyond the far end of the valley is Lee Bay (not to be confused with Lee Bay to the west of Ilfracombe), with Lee Abbey a little way inland. Constructed in 1850, this extensive building was never an abbey; it is now operated by the Anglican church as a conference and study centre.

Lynton was the terminus of the Lynton and Barnstaple Railway, an ambitious independent narrow gauge (1' 11½") railway 19¼ miles long, connecting Lynton with the standard gauge railways at Barnstaple. After great difficulty in the construction of the line through obviously difficult terrain, it was opened in 1898, one year behind schedule. For a total of 37 years the powerful little tank engines, at first three in number, later increased to four, then five, huffed and puffed their way up and down this scenic and steeply graded line. In 1923 the Southern Railway took over the line. As traffic fell away in the era of the motor car and motor bus, the line closed in September 1935.

The Walk

Leave the car park uphill along the main road into Lynton. Turn right immediately after the church to follow a very minor road, soon with sea views. At a three-way signpost take 'North Walk Valley of the Rocks'.

The way becomes a broad, surfaced, path nicely terraced above the sea, part of the South West Coast Path. At a fork keep right, along the coast, with the spine of the rocky ridge above to the left. As the path bends left there is a spectacular view of Castle Rock ahead.

The path soon reaches the main road in the Valley of the Rocks, by a roundabout. Turn right to follow the coast path along the road. *Mother Meldrum's Cave is a short diversion to the left. Some distance on the road can be avoided by forking right along a good track, but a left turn, uphill, is then necessary to rejoin the road close to a toll house.*

Continue along the toll road, passing the entrance to Lee Abbey and with a good view of Lee Bay, below. The tea shop is easily found

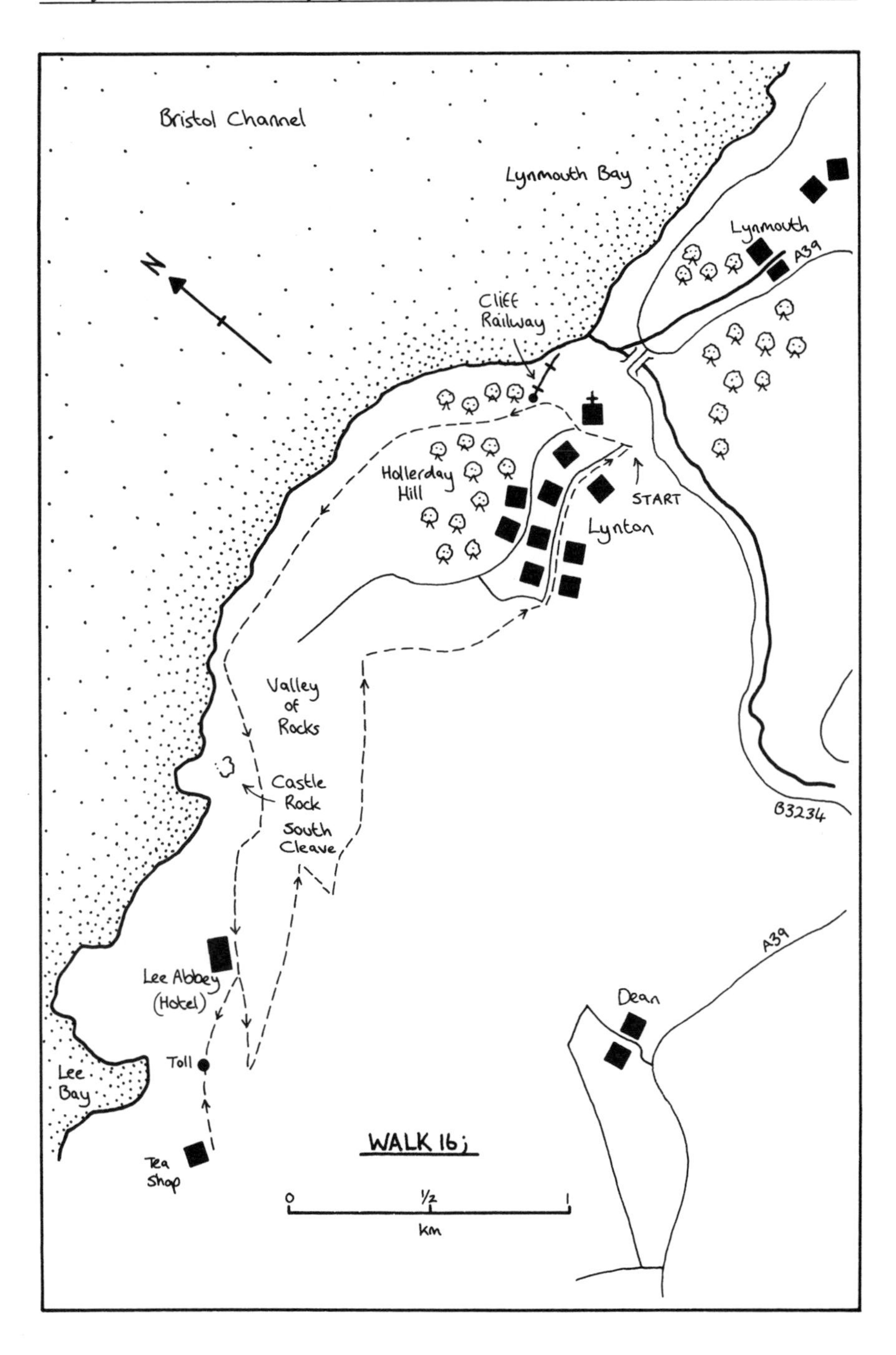
Bristol Channel
Lynmouth Bay
N
Lynmouth
A39
Cliff Railway
Hollerday Hill
START
Lynton
Valley of Rocks
Castle Rock
South Cleave
B3234
Lee Abbey (Hotel)
Toll
Lee Bay
Tea Shop
WALK 16j
0
1/2
1
km
Dean
A39

by the toll house in the bottom. Return up the road for about 400m and turn sharp right into an unmade track signposted 'Woodland walk leading to Woody Bay, Lynton over South Cliff and Six Acre Cross'. The way rises through attractive mixed woodland. Rake back sharp left at a signpost still following 'Lynton via South Cliff'.

As the track bends back right at a sharp angle, go straight on to take a lesser track which climbs the steep hillside, again with a 'Lynton via South Cliff' posting. As the path divides, keep right, uphill, continuing all the way to the top. This is South Cliff ('Cleave' on the map) and the track continues through the gorse with eventual superb views into the Valley of the Rocks.

After Lynton comes into view, turn right at a junction, still on an excellent path, now between walls. Join the public road, turning left, downhill, signposted 'Lynton¼ mile' Turn left at Crossmead then right along the main road (Lee Road) to return to the car park.

Lee Bay, Lynmouth

17. Watersmeet and The Foreland

Length: 6 miles (9.6km); a 5½ mile (8.8km) version is available.

Summary: A wonderfully varied walk combining the deep lush woodland of the East Lyn River with the high, windswept, open country of The Foreland. Two quite long ascents but, apart from some scree on The Foreland (*not included in the shortened version)*, first class underfoot.

Car Parking: Pay and display car park by the side of the main A39 road above Watersmeet. Grid reference 744488.

Map: Ordnance Survey Outdoor Leisure no. 9, Exmoor, 1:25,000. or Landranger no. 180, Barnstaple and Ilfracombe area, 1:50,000.

The Tea Shop

Although a National Trust property, access at Watersmeet is open to all. There has been a refreshment facility here since 1901 – it has long been a popular spot for walkers. Watersmeet House was originally a 19th century fishing lodge; it now houses the National Trust shop and self service café. There is only a very small indoor eating area here but this is not important as most visitors descend the valley to this beautiful area only in reasonable weather conditions. However, being in a very sheltered situation, one can almost always eat outdoors; one section has a covered veranda. The servery, although rather cramped, has a lovely atmosphere with the visitors exclaiming about the delectables such as quiche, enormous fruit pies, fruit crumbles and other temptations. Also available are soup, tea, coffee, ices, and cream teas. Open: April (Easter if earlier) to end of October from 10.30am – 5.30pm every day but closes at 4.30pm in October. Tel: 01598 753348

Watersmeet

About the area

The East Lyn River and Hoaroak Water come together at Watersmeet. Both are delightful, with waterfalls, rushing rapids and attractively diverse woodland, all set in deep valleys. As the National Trust owns most of the land, there are, literally, miles of good footpaths by the use of which the valleys can be explored.

Set strategically at the meeting place of the waters is a substantial 19th century former fishing lodge, Watersmeet House, also owned by the Trust. The house is operated as an information centre, shop, tea room and extensive tea garden.

In complete contrast is the high, windswept, open landscape of The Foreland, between Countisbury and the sea, with the lighthouse at its tip. The highest point of this area is Butter Hill at 302m (991ft). Nearby are the remains of an iron age fort.

The Walk

Go down the well-made track across the road from the car park, zig zagging down to Watersmeet House, reached over two footbridges, with fine views of the waterfalls on Hoaroak Water.

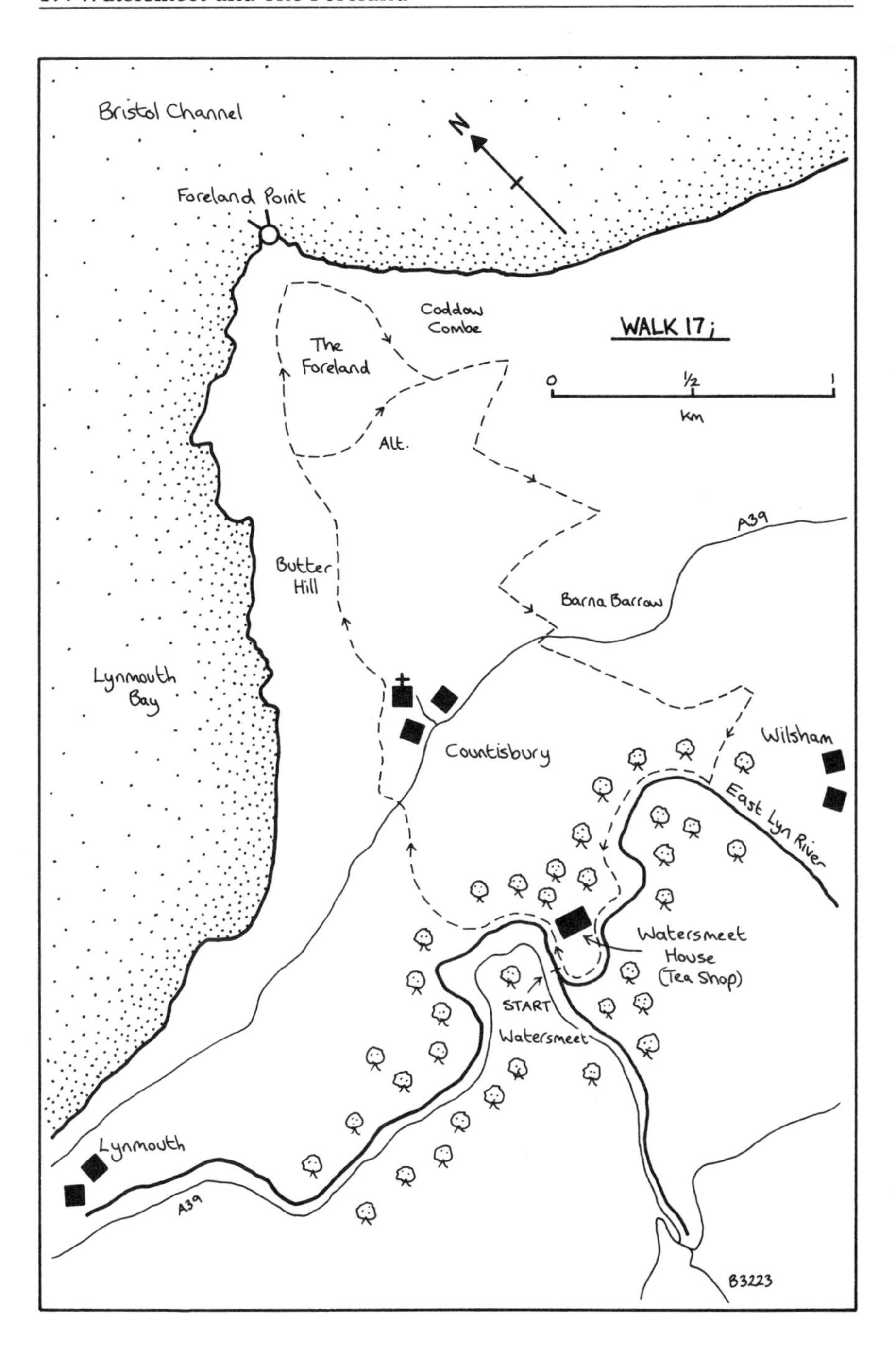
Bristol Channel
N
Foreland Point
Coddow Combe
WALK 17
The Foreland
0 ½ 1
km
Alt.
A39
Butter Hill
Barna Barrow
Lynmouth Bay
Countisbury
Wilsham
East Lyn River
Watersmeet House (Tea Shop)
START
Watersmeet
Lynmouth
A39
B3223

Turn left to follow a broad, rising, track. At a three-way signpost turn right, steeply up grass, towards 'Countisbury'. Leave the woodland through a gate and continue steeply up hill towards the A39 main road. By a three-way signpost bear left up to the road.

Go through the little gate and cross straight over the road, up steps and through another gate, signposted 'to coast path'. Keep close to the wall on the right, with Countisbury church tower now visible to the right and Lynton also very much in view. At the next signpost turn right at 'coast path' to follow the broad green track between the gorse, keeping to the coast path at further signposts.

At a three-way signpost the coast path goes to the right, signposted 'Porlock'. *Take this for the shorter version, avoiding the steep-lying scree of The Foreland.*

For the full circuit go left along a more minor path, which goes round the curve of The Foreland, descending gently towards the lighthouse. The path is narrow but adequate. Those with young children should certainly heed the warning board at the start; there are steep drops and there is some scree underfoot. Towards the end of The Foreland there is a surprise view of the coast to the east before the lighthouse is reached at Foreland Point.

Follow the lighthouse access road for the long ascent of Coddow Combe. The shorter route soon joins on the right. Near the top of the rise turn very sharply right at a 'Countisbury' signpost to take an unsurfaced track for about 1/3 mile. Where paths cross, turn left, soon reaching the National Trust car park by Barna Barrow.

Cross the main road, turn right for 40m, then left through a gate on to a bridleway signposted to 'Wilsham and Rockford'. This inviting track stays high on the side of a valley before dropping steeply to cross two small streams on footbridges. Just before the second stream turn right to take a minor path showing clearly in the undergrowth. The path stays close to the stream as it descends through woodland to the East Lyn River. There are plenty of bilberries along the way.

Turn right at the river to follow the superb path as it rises and falls for a long half mile to Watersmeet House for refreshments. Climb the zig zags back to the car park.

18. Exmoor – Doone Country

Length:	6½ miles (10.4km)
Summary:	One of the longer walks in the book, this circuit is a fine combination of the delightful valley of Badgeworthy Water and wild Exmoor moorland. Excellent underfoot but a fair amount of ascent early in the walk. Care needed with route finding on the moor.
Car Parking:	At Malmsmead. Grid reference 792478.
Map:	Ordnance Survey Outdoor Leisure no. 9, Exmoor, 1:25:000 or Landranger no. 180, Barnstaple and Ilfracombe area, 1:50,000.

The Tea Shop

The Buttery at Lorna Doone Farm is the chosen tea shop – the very name is inviting. Enthusiastically owned and managed by Graham and Lee Storey, the café is spacious and attractive. On the terrace outside there are tables with umbrellas for sunny days. Good choice on the menu – home-made soup, omelettes, delicious cakes, cream teas, and lots more. Open: 11am – 5pm every day throughout the year. Tel: 01598 741202

About the area

The Badgeworthy valley is regarded as the heart of Lorna Doone country and is very special to the hosts of admirers of R.D. Blackmore and his famous heroine, the book in question being published in 1869. This intriguing mixture of folklore and fiction is generally regarded as having a factual basis, the Doones being a notorious lawless family living on this part of Exmoor during the 16th or possibly early 17th century.

The most likely site of their habitation is close to the junction of

Hoccombe Combe and Badgeworthy Water, where the evident remains of a 'medieval' village give credence to the theory.

With or without the romance of Blackmore's story, the valley of Badgeworthy Water makes a lovely walk, with woodland and rhododendrons softening the stern Exmoor landscape. Malmsmead is the best base for the Doone country. At Lorna Doone Farm, in addition to the car park and tea shop, there is a comprehensive gift and book shop. The hamlet sits right on the boundary between Somerset and Devon, with an ancient ford across the Water accompanied by a narrow bridge, also of considerable antiquity, connecting the two counties.

Lorna Doone

The Walk

Leave Malmsmead by a broad, unmade, track which rakes back to the right of the road leading from the car park to the ford. Go uphill through a farm gate and enter Southern Wood, predominantly old sessile oak of restricted growth. Once over the top continue downhill to a minor road. Turn left and then left again to leave the road in 20m along an inviting rising track, signposted 'Brendon Common. Malmsmead Hill'

Emerge on to the open moor as the track levels out. Keep left at a point where a farm track goes off to the right, reaching a minor road

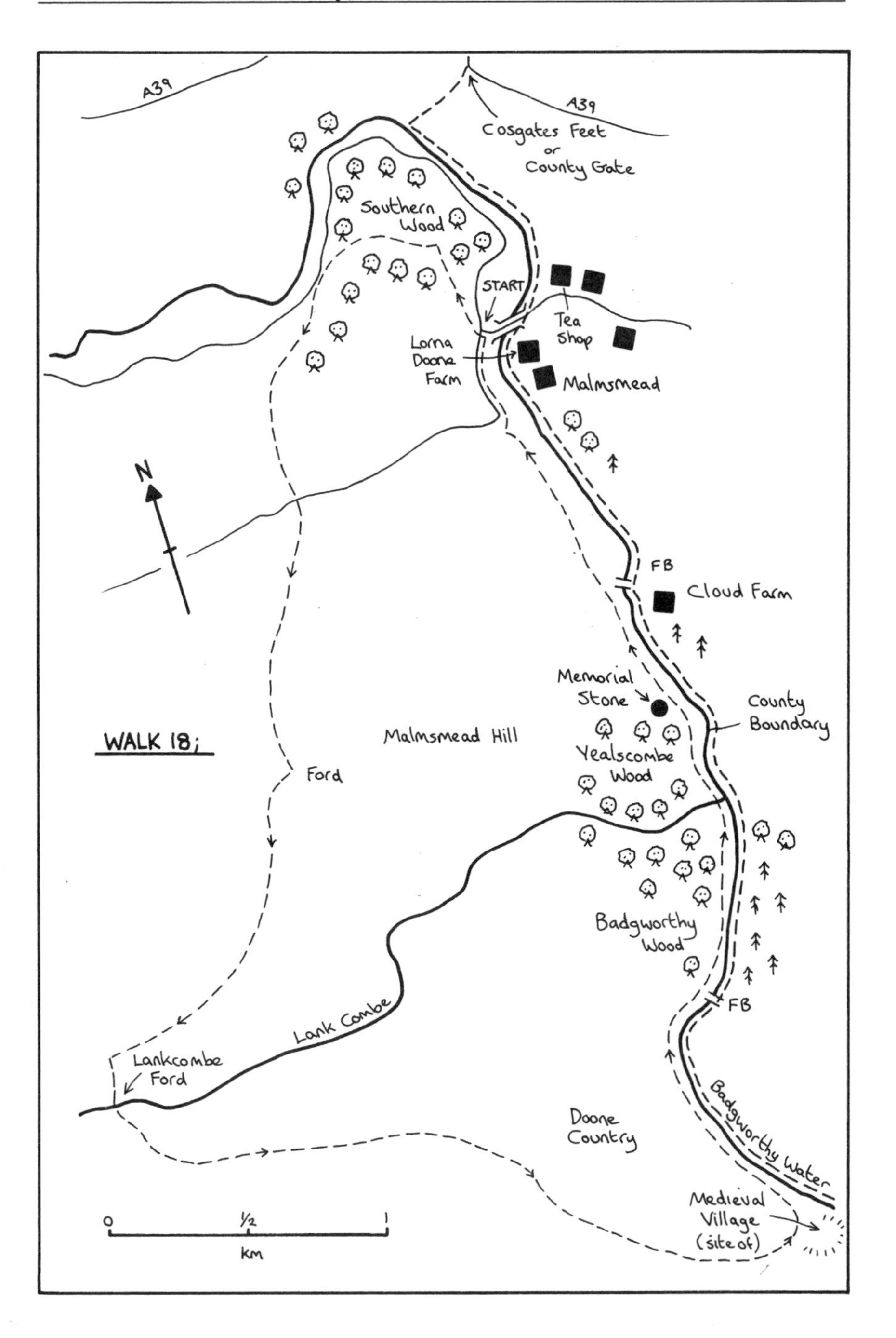
A39
A39
Cosgates Feet
or
County Gate
Southern
Wood
START
Tea
Shop
Lorna
Doone
Farm
Malmsmead
N
FB
Cloud Farm
Memorial
Stone
County
Boundary
WALK 18;
Malmsmead Hill
Yealscombe
Wood
Ford
Badgworthy
Wood
FB
Lank Combe
Lankcombe
Ford
Badgworthy Water
Doone
Country
Medieval
Village
(site of)
0
½
1
km

at a gate. Go straight across, signposted 'Brendon Common and Doone Valley' into a broad stony track. Keep right at a major fork.

At a little stream with a junction and signpost go straight on, signposted 'Brendon Common and Doone Valley', soon bending to the right Go across one meeting place of paths to reach a second, more major, crossing, with a signpost. Turn left here for 'Doone Valley', descending into Lankcombe and crossing the stream by a ford.

Climb the far side of the valley, bending left to cross a grassy area. A gate in the fence ahead confirms the route. Continue in much the same direction, crossing a tiny stream. The track now becomes much more worn as it descends into Hoccombe Coombe, very much Doone country. *A slight deviation to the right is needed to visit the scant remains of a 'medieval village' – home of the Doones?*

At the adjacent three-way signpost follow ' Malmsmead', initially by ascending the little hill, rejoining the main track and turning right. A fine path now stays close to Badgeworthy Water. There are soon a few strips of woodland to soften the otherwise harsh landscape and Badgeworthy Wood is reached after crossing a tributary stream on a footbridge. The old and rather stunted oaks are brightened in spring by an array of rhododendrons and there are plentiful bilberries along the wayside. There is also a memorial to R.D. Blackmore.

Pass the end of the bridge leading to Cloud Farm and carry on towards Malmsmead. At a quiet public road turn right to walk the last few metres to the hamlet, by hedgerows bright with campion and stitchwort.

19. Challacombe

Length: 2¼ miles (3.6km)

Summary: An easy but entirely pleasant little walk from an attractive village to its distant church and back by a different route, using well established footpaths and bridleways. All are good underfoot, with just a little roadside walking.

Car Parking: Adequate roadside spaces by the side of the road through the village, close to the Methodist chapel. Grid reference 693408.

Map: Ordnance Survey Outdoor Leisure no. 9, Exmoor, 1:25:000 or Landranger no. 180, Barnstaple and Ilfracombe area, 1:50,000.

The Tea Shop

"Owls Roost" was a surprise find at the end of a busy walking day; it was then necessary to find a suitable short walk in order to include this very homely tea-room. Mrs Whitehead has been running the tea room in the family home for seventeen years and visitors return again and again.

Prices are very reasonable – the cream teas are enormous (so make sure that you do the walk first!). The scones and cakes are home-made and of superb quality. Sandwiches, ploughman's lunch with Cheddar or Stilton, toasted sandwiches, are also available.

There is a choice of Darjeeling, Assam, or Earl Grey tea. The tea cosies (unusual to provide them these days) match the attractively patterned china. One very thoughtful idea is to provide an extra tea bag for those who prefer stronger tea. Open: Easter to the end of the autumn half term holiday, 10.30am – 6pm every day except Fridays when opening is not until 3pm. Tel: 01598 763452

About the area

On the western fringe of Exmoor, Challacombe village extends thinly for some distance alongside the tiny River Bray, crossed by an apparent packhorse bridge. One end of the village is on the Blackmoor Gate to Simonsbath road (B3358), where there is a filling station, shop and post office.

About one mile distant, at the farming hamlet of Barton Town, is the parish church of Holy Trinity. Apart from the tower, the church was rebuilt in 1850. Inside are an ancient font and an access stairway which passes under an arch to reach the pulpit. It seems likely that the outward part of this walk would be the ancient path by which generations of villagers went to and from their church.

About three miles to the south west, by the side of the Blackmoor Gate to South Molton road (A399), the Exmoor Steam Railway and Gardens provides 'fun and nostalgia for the family' during the season. The principal feature is a narrow gauge railway line operated by steam locomotives.

The Walk

From the vicinity of the Methodist chapel go south west to the little old (packhorse?) bridge. Turn right at Home Place Farm, signposted 'Challacombe Church'. Go through two gates, pass another signpost and a small caravan site.

Pass yet another signpost to reach a small gate. As the track appears to fork, keep left, down to a bridge over a stream. Continue through more gates and stiles along an unmistakable track hugging the bottom edge of the steeply rising woodland of Barton Plantation.

At a three-way signpost turn right to 'Challacombe Church', entering the woodland at a gate and rising. Emerge at a gate with signpost and follow the indicated line across two meadows. Go through a gate, cross a rough stony lane and head for the obvious church, entering the churchyard at an iron gate. The church has apparent structural problems.

Exit by the lych gate and turn right, uphill, at the public road. In less than 100m turn right at a signpost 'Bridleway to Withecombe

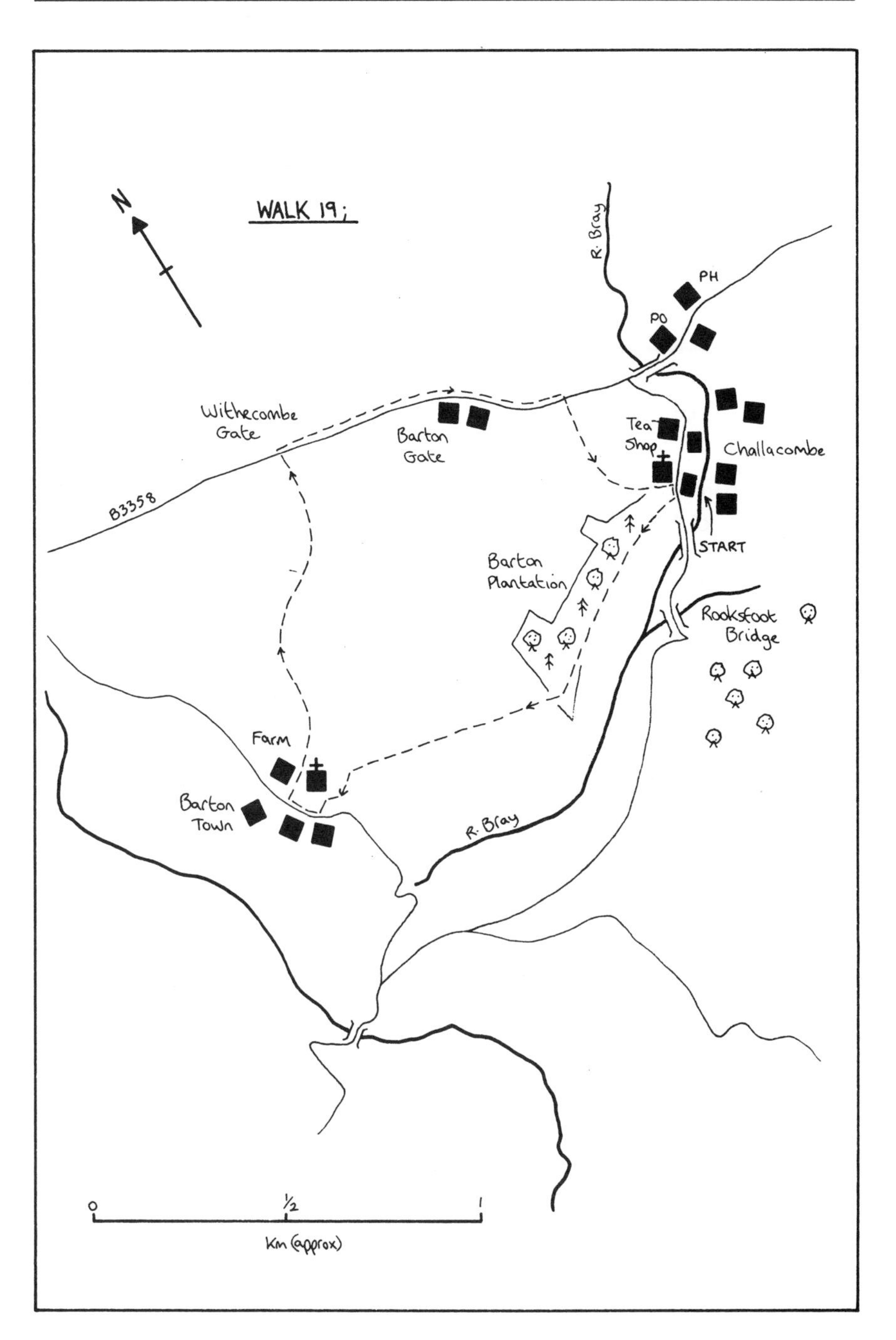
N
WALK 19;
R. Bray
PH
PO
Withecombe
Gate
Barton
Gate
Tea
Shop
Challacombe
B3358
START
Barton
Plantation
Rooksfoot
Bridge
Farm
Barton
Town
R. Bray
0
½
1
Km (approx)

Gate' Go through two farm gates, keeping to the right of the farm itself. At an apparent junction go straight ahead, uphill, over grass between hedgebanks.

At the top go through a farm gate on the right and keep close to the hedgebank on the left. Go through another gate and angle right, between wide spaced banks, with superb views across to high Exmoor. Go downhill to a gate at the bottom and continue to another obvious gate in the far right corner of a field, giving access to the B3358 road. Turn right and walk along the roadside back towards Challacombe.

As the village is approached, just over a brow, turn right, through the second of two adjacent farm gates, with a 'footpath' sign. Keep close to the hedgebank on the right, go through a small gate and continue downhill to two gates giving access to the minor road through the village. Turn left to walk past the car parking and the Methodist chapel to the tea room. Return to your car.

Challacombe

20. Arlington Court

Length: 3 miles (4.8km)

Summary: A ramble round the Arlington Court estate, largely in woodland, but with some farmland to add variety. The rise and fall is quite considerable but the gradients are generally reasonable. Although just a little mud is possible, this is one walk for which walking boots are not strictly necessary. When the property is open to the public, access is through the ticket office/shop and, except for members of the National Trust, payment for entry to the gardens is required. When the property is closed, access is through the small gate at the side of the ticket office.

Car Parking: Official car park for Arlington Court. Grid reference 614407.

Map: Ordnance Survey Outdoor Leisure no., Exmoor, 1:25,000 or Landranger no. 180, Barnstaple and Ilfracombe area, 1:50,000.

The Tea Shop

Popular catering here! A main restaurant with waitress service (probably not the most suitable choice if still wearing walking boots). However, the counter-service tea room is bustling and has a very adequate choice of food at all times of day including, of course, Devon cream tea. For sunny days there is a pleasant, sheltered, patio with sun umbrellas. So, there's everything here: indoors and outdoors, from full meals to ice creams. Open: April (or Easter if earlier) to end of October 11am – 5pm every day but closed on Saturdays except Bank Holidays. If in doubt, telephone first. Tel. 01271 850296. Note: To access the tea facility it is necessary to pay admission to the grounds if not members of The National Trust.

About the area

The present house at Arlington Court, constructed in 1820-23, is the third on the site. Home of the Chichester family for more than 500 years, the estate was handed over to the National Trust in 1949, following the death of Miss Rosalie Chichester whose home it had been for 84 years.

Inside the house are collections of many kinds, including pictures, whilst the nearby stable block has an array of 19th century carriages and other horse-drawn vehicles; carriage rides along the drive are a particular feature. The gardens and grounds are attractive and comprehensive. Sir John Chichester dammed the River Yeo in 1850 to create a sizeable lake which is now rich in wildlife, particularly water fowl. There are hides for observation. Sir John also planned a new entrance drive to the house, crossing the lake by a suspension bridge. The piers were constructed, but after his death in 1851, the project was left incomplete. On the course of the walk is an obelisk marking the site of a bonfire on 21st June 1887, celebrating Queen Victoria's Silver Jubilee. Closer to the house, Jacob's sheep and Shetland ponies may be seen.

The nearby church has undergone extensive renovation work but the 15th century tower remains.

The normal National Trust opening season applies.

The Walk

From the car park walk down to the ticket office or gate as appropriate and continue along a gravelled drive. Before the house turn right at a signpost ' walk to the lake 1 mile. follow the drive'. Keep to the same drive, passing another 'lake' signpost. The woodland has mature trees and large rhododendrons, carpeted with bluebells in Spring.

Home Farm, with its ornate chimneys, is soon approached. Look for the stone herons on gate pillars, obviously a family emblem. Go left here; there is another 'lake' sign. Ignore a waymark and pass along an avenue of 'monkey puzzle' trees. On this section there are long views of upland farming country, pleasant rather than exiting.

Heron, Arlington Court

Back in woodland, there is a short, signposted diversion to the right to reach a hide by one end of the lake, which is a Site of Special Scientific Interest. Back at the junction, head for 'lake and Yeo valley'. The lake is soon in view on the right; at this point there is a memorial urn to Rosalie Caroline Chichester.

Go to the dam at the foot; one of the piers for the proposed suspension bridge can be seen near the head of the lake. Bear left after the dam, then right and left, to head for 'Loxhore and deer park'. The track is now beside the River Yeo. At a three-way signpost take 'Loxhore and Deer Park Wood', cross the River Yeo at Tucker's Bridge and turn left.

At another three-way sign follow 'Arlington Court and Loxhore via Deer Park Wood'. Commence the long, steady, rise back along the valley side, with the tumbling stream to the left, below. There are more 'Arlington' signposts. Rise steeply to a gate and out into more open countryside. Go over grass, then along a row of over-mature beech trees, soon with some long views.

Pass by the obelisk, go through a gate and turn right (waymark), to go up the edge of a field to a waymarked gate. Turn left through the gate and pass through a small area of woodland, well carpeted with bluebells and red campion. At a surfaced roadway turn left, then left again before the stable block building. The church is to the right as the road descends to the house and gardens. The tea shop and garden is to the right of the main building. Return to the car park by the ticket office/shop or gate.

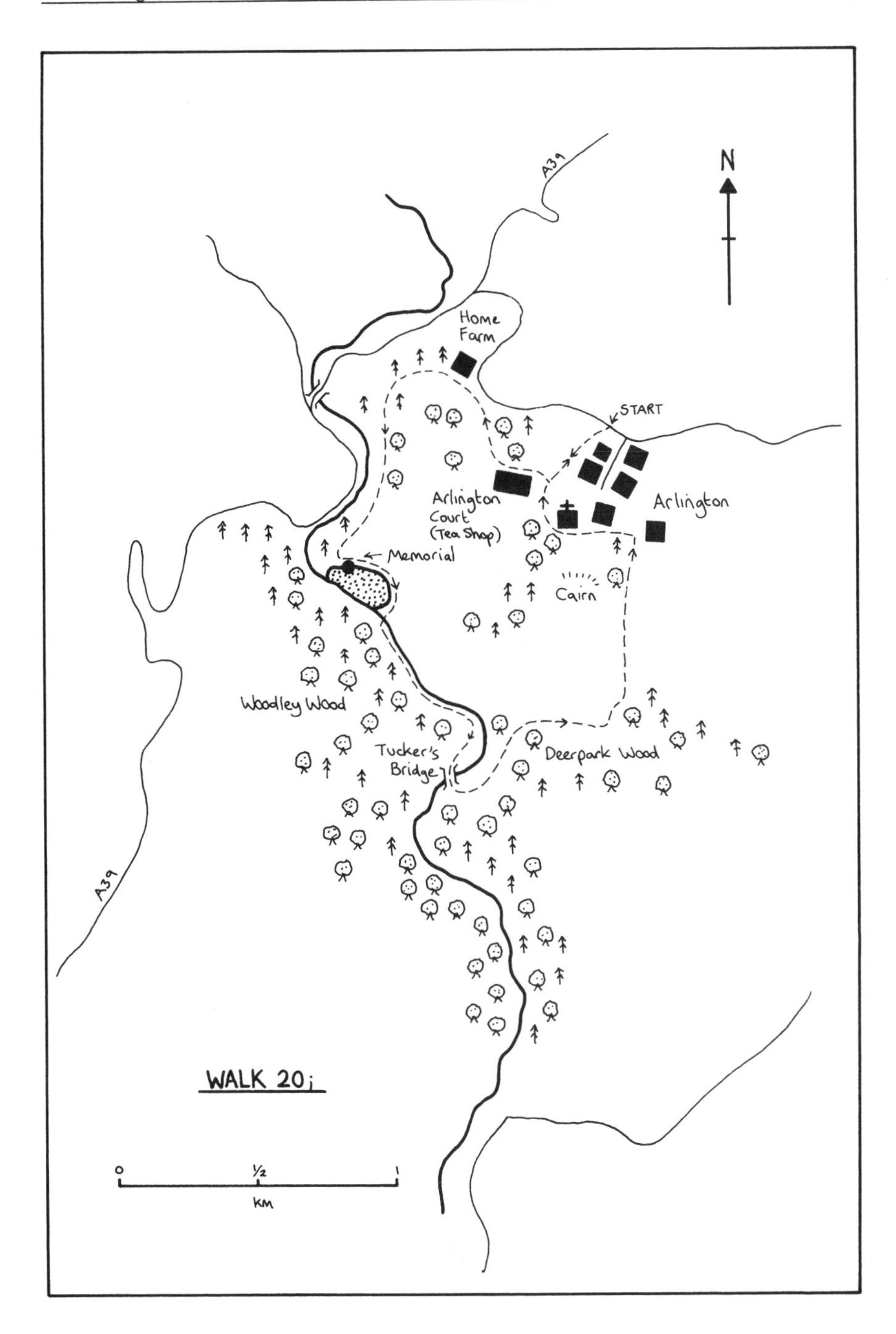
A39
N
Home Farm
START
Arlington Court (Tea Shop)
Arlington
Memorial
Cairn
Woodley Wood
Tucker's Bridge
Deerpark Wood
A39
WALK 20
0
½
1
KM

21. West Down

Length: 4¾ miles (7.6km)

Summary: A walk through farming country, close to the busy visitor honeypots of the coast, but entirely quiet. Largely upland, with some long views There is a fair amount of rise and fall and some of the rights of way are not well marked on the ground.

Car Parking: West Down village is short of suitable parking places. An informal lay-by by the side of a lane leading towards Rock Hill and West Hill is best. Grid reference 517419.

Map: Ordnance Survey Outdoor Leisure no. 9, Exmoor, 1:25,000 or Landranger no. 180, Barnstaple and Ilfracombe, 1:25,000.

The Tea Shop

The Long House Tea Room at West Down is highly recommended. The service is pleasant and friendly – Martyn and Yvonne Lavender are always pleased to chat to customers and to share their enthusiasm and knowledge of North Devon. The menu has huge temptations such as the cheese tea – local farmhouse cheese with cheese scones and Devon chutney or try the apple pie tea with Devonshire clotted cream. Toasted tea cakes, sandwiches, home-made cakes, are also served. Each day the "dish of the day" is served at lunch time.

En-suite rooms available for bed and breakfast; there is a good inn opposite where evening meals can be taken. Open: 10.30am – 5.30pm everyday from Easter to end of October. Tel: 01271 863242

About the area

Quite close to the main A361 road, but nevertheless essentially a quiet backwater, West Down village is largely unspoilt. The church was largely rebuilt in the 17th and 18th centuries but does have a 14th century south transept and a north transept roof of the same

Church, West Down

age. The font is Norman. The village has an inn, post office/stores and tea shop.

The Walk

From the lay-by head towards the village centre, turn right at the nearby junction, then right again at the next junction, signposted 'Aylescott'. Descend to cross a stream at Roborough Bridge. Go over a stile on the left and up by the hedge to two more stiles before rejoining the road.

Continue along the road, past a junction, to Lower Aylescott. As the road bends sharp right, go straight on into an unmade lane with a 'public footpath' sign. Negotiate a gate, an awkward stile and a small boggy area before crossing a stream. Rise at a steady gradient on a wide track, with woodland on the right.

The farm on the hillside opposite is Crackaway Barton. The track peters out at the foot of a long, narrow, rising meadow. The Ordnance Survey shows the right of way by the hedge on the right, but follow any cattle-worn line through the grass which makes the going easier.

Exit by the gate at the top and go to the public road at Burland Cross. Go straight across, over a signposted stile, then left descending along the edge of a cultivated field. Go over or through a tied up gate and continue close to the hedge on the left to a stile in the bottom corner, giving access to a road.

Turn right for 350m and, after passing two houses, turn sharp left into a very minor road, first dropping to the valley bottom, then rising to Bittadon. At a three-way 'public footpath' sign by the gateway to Bittadon Barton go straight on. There is a tiny church to the right, above.

Continue past Bittadon Cottages, now on a stony track. Turn left through a gate at another 'public footpath' sign and keep close to the fence on the right. Go over a waymarked stile, then turn right, through the hedge, at a yellow arrow on a post, turning left at once to continue the previous line. There is a fair amount of cattle-churned ground hereabouts.

After two more stiles pass across the bottom edge of the garden of

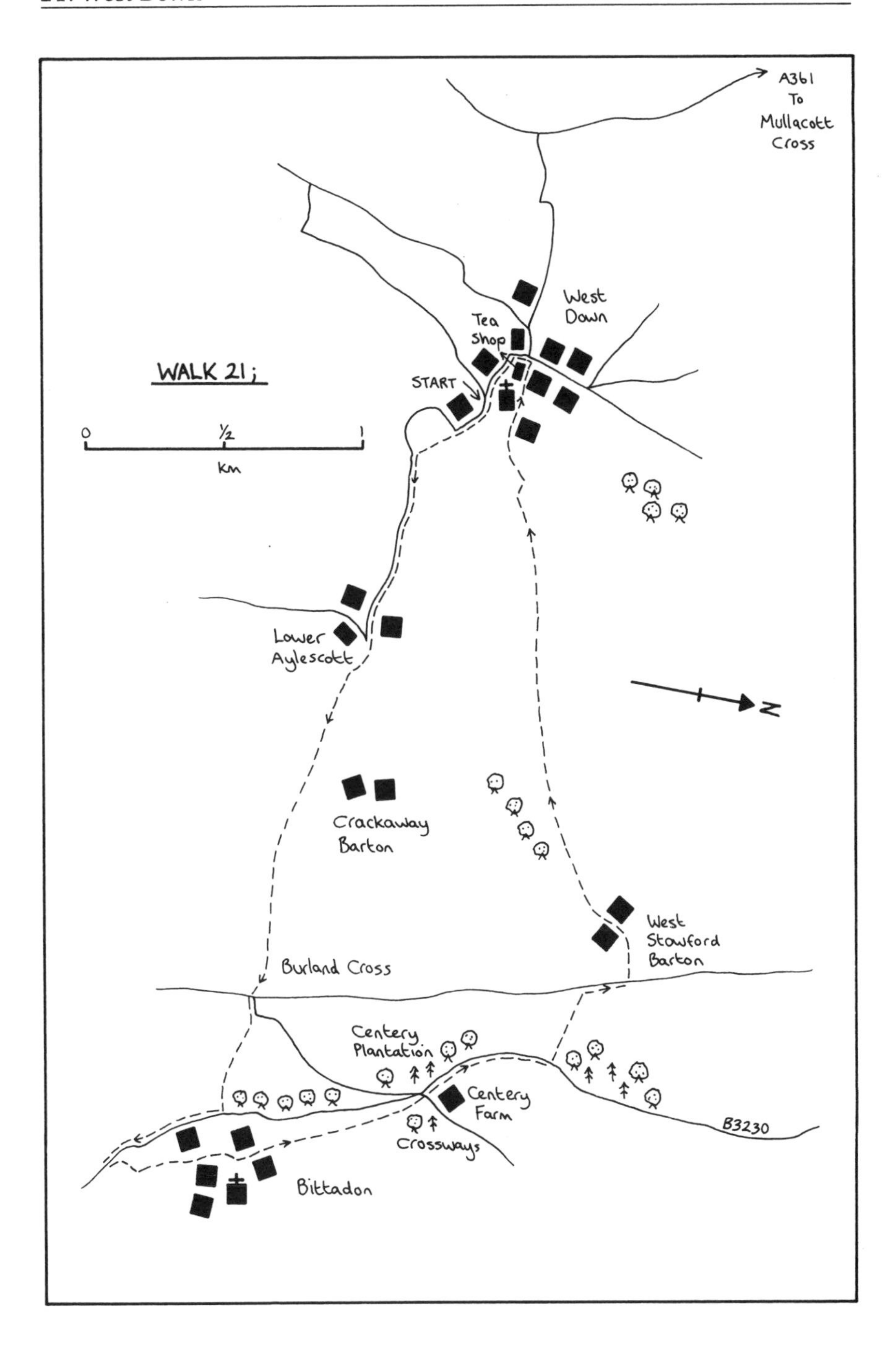
A361
To
Mullacott
Cross
West
Down
Tea
Shop
WALK 21;
START
0
½
1
Km
N
Lower
Aylescott
Crackaway
Barton
West
Stowford
Barton
Burland Cross
Centery
Plantation
Centery
Farm
Crossways
B3230
Bittadon

Crossways and go over a stile to join a minor road. Turn left to reach the more important road. Turn right along this road for nearly one third of a mile. Centery Farm with its pond, below, is quite pretty.

Look out for a public footpath sign and turn left over a broken gate. The indicated right of way goes straight across a large field but, if there is a tall growing crop, you may prefer to keep to the field edge on the right. Exit at a gate in the far right corner and turn right along the minor road for a short distance.

Turn left along the drive to West Stowford Barton ('public footpath' sign). Pass the farm (yellow arrow) to a gate at the far end. Bear left (yellow arrow) at the next gate and follow a farm trackway. Rise to cross a large meadow; the line is a little south of west and farm vehicle tracks may initially be helpful. As the crest is reached aim for the right hand end of a distant outgrown hedge.

Go through a gate in a hedge in a dip and keep the same line, crossing an area known as Twitching Park Cleaves, before reaching a gate to the right of the outgrown hedge. Go across a stony lane to a 'public footpath' sign and stile opposite. West Down can now be seen ahead, about half a mile away. Keep a wall/hedge on the right to reach a waymarked gate and two more stiles, then over a stone stile and on towards the church spire. There is another stone stile before taking a diagonal line across a field to a gate/stile in the bottom left corner, then an unsurfaced lane leading into the village over a mini ford with footbridge.

At a road junction go right, along the village street, to the tea shop. From the tea shop go past the post office and church before turning right into the minor road with the parking lay-by.

22. Great Torrington

Length: 3¾ miles (6km)

Summary: A remarkable little walk combining Torrington Common, the former railway line, the Rolle Canal and Castle Hill to go three quarters of the way round the little town of Great Torrington. Although the route is never more than one mile from the town centre, the built-up area is out of sight for the great majority of the way. First class paths, many being surfaced. Quite steep ascent of Castle Hill at the end of the walk.

Car Parking: Pay and display car park off South Street, to the south of the town centre. Grid reference 495190.

Map: Ordnance Survey Landranger no. 180, Barnstaple and Ilfracombe area, 1:50,000.

The Tea Shop

Jennifer and Colin Brown, the proprietors of "Browns", enjoy living in Devon and running this smart delicatessen. The tea room, situated behind the shop, is small and attractive. Open for morning coffee, lunches, and afternoon teas. The menu is very tempting – cooked meals such as turkey sausages in red wine and cranberry sauce, or courgette and cream cheese bake. From the chiller cabinet one can choose quiche, or from a variety of cooked meats. For something a little lighter there is home-made pate with toast. The freshly made scones with jam and cream can certainly be recommended. Drinks include a cafétière of coffee, pot of tea with a choice of blend, fruit teas, and herbal tea. Open: 10am – 4pm daily throughout the year but closed Sundays and Bank Holidays. Tel: 01805 622900

About the area

On three sides. Great Torrington is a hill-top town, perching above the deep valleys of the River Torridge and a tributary stream. On the same three sides, there is extensive open common. A 14th century castle once stood on Castle Hill but has long gone, apparently even before the civil war brought strife to this part of Devon. The castellated walls now apparent were constructed in 1846. The best known and most tragic event of the civil war followed a battle in 1646 which effectively ended the Royalist resistance in Devon. Unknown to the Parliamentarian commanding officer, the church was in use as a gunpowder store. Two hundred Royalist prisoners were confined in the church when there was a huge explosion, with great loss of life. The church of St Michael and All Angels was rebuilt in 1651 and has since been further renovated. Musical concerts are held during the season.

An ambitious enterprise in 1823 was the construction of the Rolle canal to connect Town Mills, below Torrington, with the navigable River Torridge at Landcross, and thence Bideford and the sea. The canal closed in 1871, as roads were improved and railways arrived, but much of it is still evident, part being used in this walk. The sec-

Taddiport Bridge, Torrington

tion between Town Mills and Taddiport became a toll road. The toll house by Taddiport Bridge can still be seen.

Torrington's first railway was a 3ft (0.9m) gauge line, the Marland Light Railway, with a wooden viaduct across the river. In 1872, when the London and South Western Railway (later the Southern Railway) extended their line from Barnstaple and Bideford, passenger trains reached the town. The wooden viaduct was replaced by the present steel and concrete structure in 1925. The line closed in the mid 1980s and has been developed for walkers and cyclists as part of the 'Tarka Trail'.

Today, the compact town centre bustles around a small square and the attractions include the Plough Arts Centre and a local history museum, with tourist information close by. On the edge of town the Dartington Glass factory offers tours of the glass making process for visitors and a 'factory shop' complex has grown up on the site. Outside the town, most important is Rosemoor Gardens, a wonderful horticultural display managed by the Royal Horticultural Society. Close to Rosemoor the 'Great Torrington Railway' offers rides on a miniature line.

The Walk

From the car park turn left along South Street. Bear right at Halsdon Terrace, then left at the main road (New Street) for 200m. Turn right at Stoneman's Lane. This soon becomes a real lane, still surfaced, as it descends quite steeply.

Go straight on at a junction and continue down to a stile, then a foot bridge over a stream. Angle right, uphill, through lush undergrowth, to a few steps and a more major path. Turn left and walk along the Common, here an attractively gorse covered valley side with a variety of footpaths.

Keep straight on at a junction with a major rising track, soon passing behind a few houses. Bear slightly right to cross a large meadow on a distinct path. At the far end turn, left to head for a stile at the bottom corner. Go over, to join the trackbed of the former railway line. Turn left, soon reaching the former station, now the 'Puffing Billy' inn, with beer garden, ice cream stall and cycle hire.

Follow the track under the bridge which carries the main road and turn left into a little opening immediately before the viaduct which carried the line across the Torridge. *A diversion for a few metres on to the viaduct is recommended.*

Go over a stile on the right and descend steps to a broad track below. This is the bed of the old Rolle Canal. Turn left to walk on the level to the huge creamery factory. The right of way goes straight through, between buildings, to reach a road by Taddiport Bridge, with the former toll house opposite.

Cross the road to a 'public footpath' sign and continue along the line of the old canal, passing an outstanding bank of valerian of both red varieties. In not much more than 100m fork left up a surfaced footpath which climbs Castle Hill at a steady gradient, with plenty of seats along the way. The obelisk in view commemorates the Battle of Waterloo. At the top is a belvedere with wonderful views over the Torridge valley, including Rosemoor Gardens, Town Mills and the site of the former Leper Colony at Taddiport.

Turn left along the surfaced path beneath the sham castellated wall for less than 100m and turn right into the car park. The tea shop may already have been spotted in South Street just to the left from the car park entrance.

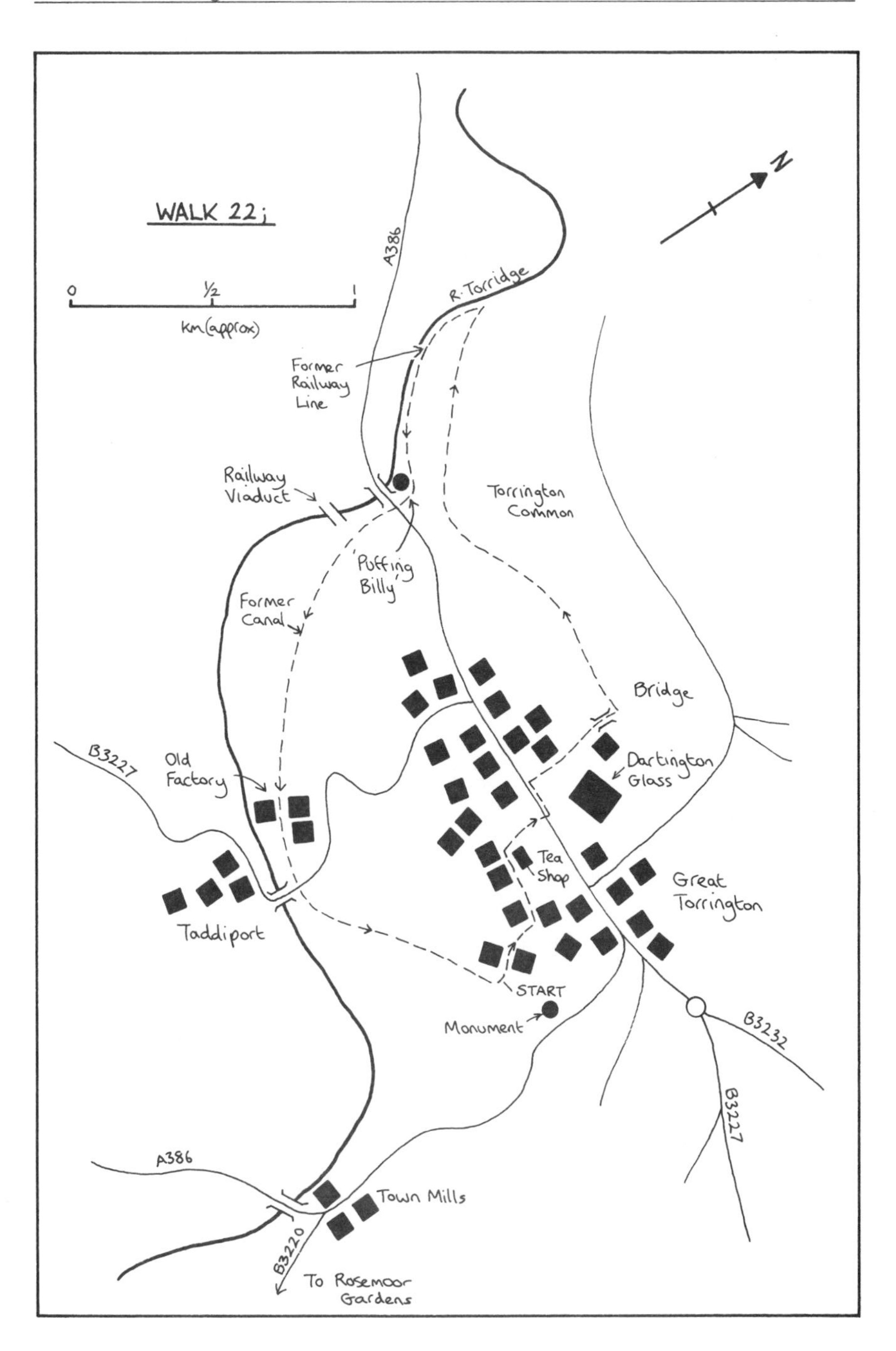
WALK 22;
N
0
½
1
km (approx)
A386
R. Torridge
Former
Railway
Line
Railway
Viaduct
Torrington
Common
Puffing
Billy
Former
Canal
Bridge
B3227
Old
Factory
Dartington
Glass
Tea
Shop
Great
Torrington
Taddiport
START
Monument
B3232
B3227
A386
Town Mills
B3220
To Rosemoor
Gardens

23. Chittlehampton and Umberleigh

Length: 6¼ miles (10km)

Summary: A walk in the heart of rural Devon, linking the beautiful Taw valley and a fine upland village, with woodland and farming country. There is a fair amount of ascent and not all rights of way are obvious on the ground. Part of the route is along quiet minor roads.

Car Parking: Informal parking close to the railway station and village hall in Umberleigh. Grid reference 609238.

Map: Ordnance Survey Landranger no. 180, Barnstaple and Ilfracombe area, 1:50,000.

The Tea Shop

"Cobbles" was one of those hoped for but unexpected finds – a tea shop in a delightful off-the-beaten track Devonshire village. Newly opened in 1997 by Nigel and Joan Sinclair, Cobbles is open for morning coffee, lunches, and afternoon teas. home-made scones are served with clotted cream and two kinds of jam; there is a choice of sandwiches, toast with pate, and the daily "specials" are chalked up on the blackboard. Interesting collectibles are displayed and can be purchased. The proprietors are only too happy to demonstrate the antique wind-up gramophone. Open 11am – 5pm every day from March to the end of October. However, subject to demand hours may change. It is possible that Cobbles will open in the winter months. Suggest telephone first. Tel: 01769 540304

About the area

The tower of the parish church at Chittlehampton is regarded as the finest in Devon, its height of 114ft (35m) emphasised by its position at the top of the lovely little square at the heart of this large and attractive village. The site of the church was formerly a place of pil-

Cottages, Chittlehampton

grimage to the shrine of St Urith, martyred nearby. Inside the church is a richly carved stone pulpit, beautiful windows and much more of interest.

For today's needs in Chittlehampton there are Post Office/stores, inn, public conveniences and, of course, a tea shop. About two miles from Chittlehampton, is the well signposted Cobbaton Combat Vehicle Museum, including tanks and armoured vehicles from World War II, a personal collection which has grown like Topsy and is open to the public during the season. Not much more than a hamlet, Umberleigh sits in the bottom of the Taw valley with river, railway and road close together. As in the case of Eggesford (walk no. 26) the functioning railway station is perhaps the most important feature although there is also a café.

The Walk

From Umberleigh station walk towards the fine bridge over the River Taw. Turn sharp right along the front of an engineering works. There is a signpost partly concealed in a tall hedge. Go through a gate then an area used as the works dumping ground, after which there is a proper riverside path.

Go under the angled railway bridge, a utilitarian metal structure on wide stone piers, indicating that the previous bridge carried a double track railway line. The path stays close to the swift running waters of the River Taw for about half a mile. When a few buildings become visible fairly close on the right, slant away from the river towards a farm gate. Go through and then, in a few metres, turn right at a waymarked stile to rise along a grassy little lane to the public road. Turn right, pass Hoe Farm, and in 100m or so look for a 'public footpath' sign in the hedge on the left. Go over what should be a stile and head uphill across the field to a waymarked gate in the boundary hedge.

From here head for Whey Farm ahead, via a gap in the fence at the far left corner of the field. The grass hereabouts might be rather long. Go through a farm gate to reach a minor road. Turn left, then right at a junction, to head for Chittlehampton along the quiet road, obviously better for walkers than for the drivers of Reliant Robin cars.

Pass Watergate, join a more major road, bending slightly right, and turn left at the crossroads in the village. The tea shop faces the church across the square. Leave the tea shop, turning right. In 40m turn right at a public footpath sign to take a well-used village path through a gate and on tarmac across a field. Most unusually, go under part of a house to join a public road. Turn left, then cross a main road at Homedown Cross, heading for Chittlehamholt along a surfaced lane. As the lane rises and bends left, go through a farm gate on the right with a 'public footpath' sign to follow a broad farm track. Continue the same line along the edge of a ploughed field to a gate and a potentially boggy area. Go straight on along the side of the fence.

Cross the next meadow to a waymarked double stile and carry on to double farm gates at the far end of a very large meadow, with

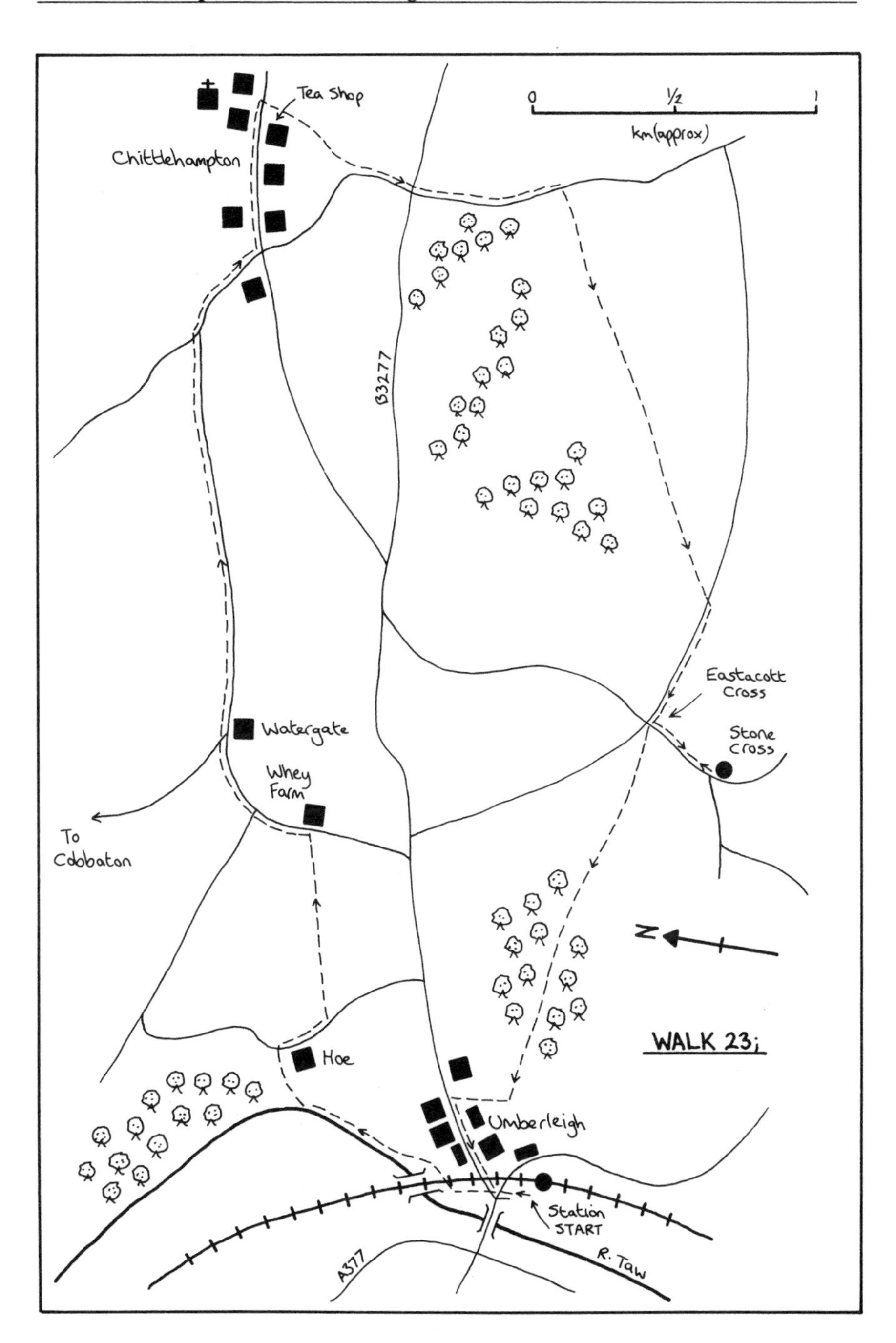
Tea Shop
0
1/2
1
km (approx)
Chittlehampton
B3277
Eastacott Cross
Stone Cross
Watergate
Whey Farm
To Cobbaton
WALK 23;
Hoe
Umberleigh
Station START
A377
R. Taw

woodland below on the right. There are good views back to Chittlehampton with its dominant church tower. After two more gates pass an agricultural building on the left to reach a minor road. Turn right to Eastacott Cross. *Here, a diversion of about 150m to the left is recommended to visit a fine ancient cross at Stonecross road junction.*

Back on course, go down the tarmac lane with a 'public footpath' sign to a hamlet. As the road bends into the hamlet go straight on to enter woodland at a broken gate with yellow arrow. The distinct path continues downhill through the woods, with plenty of bluebells and primroses in Spring.

On approaching the far end in about ⅓ mile, go right at a fork, then over a stile and down the right edge of a small field to a gate. Umberleigh is now visible ahead. Join a rudimentary lane, turning right. Pass a farm and follow the surfaced drive to the public road, turning left to return to the parking area.

24. South Molton

Distance: 3¼ miles (5.5km)

Summary: A pleasant circuit including the middle of South Molton and a little of the valley of the River Mole, with Range Woods. Rise and fall is moderate and much of the way is along the quiet backwater of Grilstone Lane. There is some roadside walking at either end of the route.

Car Parking: Large car park (pay and display on Thursday, market day, only), behind the Market Hall in the town centre. Grid reference, 715257.

Map: Ordnance Survey Landranger no. 180, Barnstaple and Ilfracombe, 1:25,000.

The Tea Shop

The Parlour is a chosen member of The Tea Council's Guild of Tea Shops; it is a recent award winner. This is definitely one for the connoisseur as well as those merely in need of sustenance. The teas offered are all leaf (presented with individual strainers), and include Assam, Keeman from China, Uva, Oolong Fancy, and many others. Advice about choice of tea will be willingly given. Food includes all day breakfast, cream teas, sandwiches, and old-fashioned favourites such as sardines on toast, crumpets, toast with cinnamon butter or marmite. Decor is most interesting – just as the name implies, the tea room is a parlour, furnished and finished in Victorian style. Open: 10am – 5pm, Tuesday – Saturday all the year. However, usually closed for a few weeks during the winter period. Tel: 01769 574144.

About the area

Since the North Devon relief road has taken the great weight of holiday traffic to and from North Devon and Cornwall away from the town, South Molton has reverted to being a friendly market town,

Near South Molton

the centre of a substantial area which is predominantly rural; a town of more importance than its actual size would indicate. Early prosperity was founded on the wool trade; there has been an annual Sheep Fair since 1357. Overlying its basic functions, the town is strong on providing for visitors, with a high proportion of antique shops and refreshments of all types. The town hall of 1740, a handsome Georgian building, contains the museum, with a lively local display. Geology and mining are also featured.

Across the way from the town hall, the spacious church of St Michael has a great 15th century tower. At the Barnstaple end of the town the Quince Honey Farm claims to be the world's largest and most famous honey bee exhibition. The comprehensive display (open to visitors during the season) includes a video show, café and picnic areas. The shop is open throughout the year. The surrounding countryside is comparatively gentle.

The Walk

From the car park set off in an easterly (facing the church tower, go to the right) direction, through a little gateway, with the swimming pool to the right. Go through a children's play area, with public conveniences to the right. Exit through a gate to a main road, turning right to walk past Summerfield's supermarket. Turn left into Poltimore Road and then turn right into Oakhayes.

Pass garages to follow a signposted footpath, soon reaching a flight of steps. Ascend to a main road, turning left, downhill. There is a roadside pavement and the road is not usually very busy. There are compensating views towards Exmoor.

Continue along the road, with the River Mole below to the left, until after the ending of the pavement. Range Woods fall away steeply below. The drive to a house named Lynwood is reached, on the right. In a further 30m turn left to go down concrete steps with a 'footpath' signpost and follow a delightful path through Range Woods, descending gently among the dominant spruce and larch, with some oak and plenty of bluebells on the lower margin of the trees. Grey squirrels are usually apparent hereabouts.

At a fork head left on the more minor path. Go over a stile and, at the lower fringe of the woodland, turn left to a footbridge. Cross the River Mole here and go over a stile into Grilstone Lane. *To the right is a bridge over the River Yeo; the confluence of the two rivers can be seen 100m or so downstream*

Turn left up Grilstone Lane to ascend gradually between hedge banks adorned with stitchwort, campion, herb robert, cow parsley, buttercups, honeysuckle and dandelions. Pass a farm, then the house, 'Grilstone'. At the top of the rise the extensive views can be enjoyed through various gateways.

Continue to a main road and turn left to return direct to South Molton. Where the road crosses the River Mole at Mole Bridge, the 'Mill on the Mole' and a large building on the other side of the road are evidence of South Molton's former water powered industrial area.

Just after the bridge there is a direct route back to the car park for walkers not wanting tea. *Fork left along Poltimore Road.* For the tea shop and the interesting town centre keep straight on along East Street, rich in antique and bric-a-brac shops, soon reaching 'The Parlour' on the left.

After tea, to return to the car park continue to the town centre and turn left under the arches by the Market Hall.

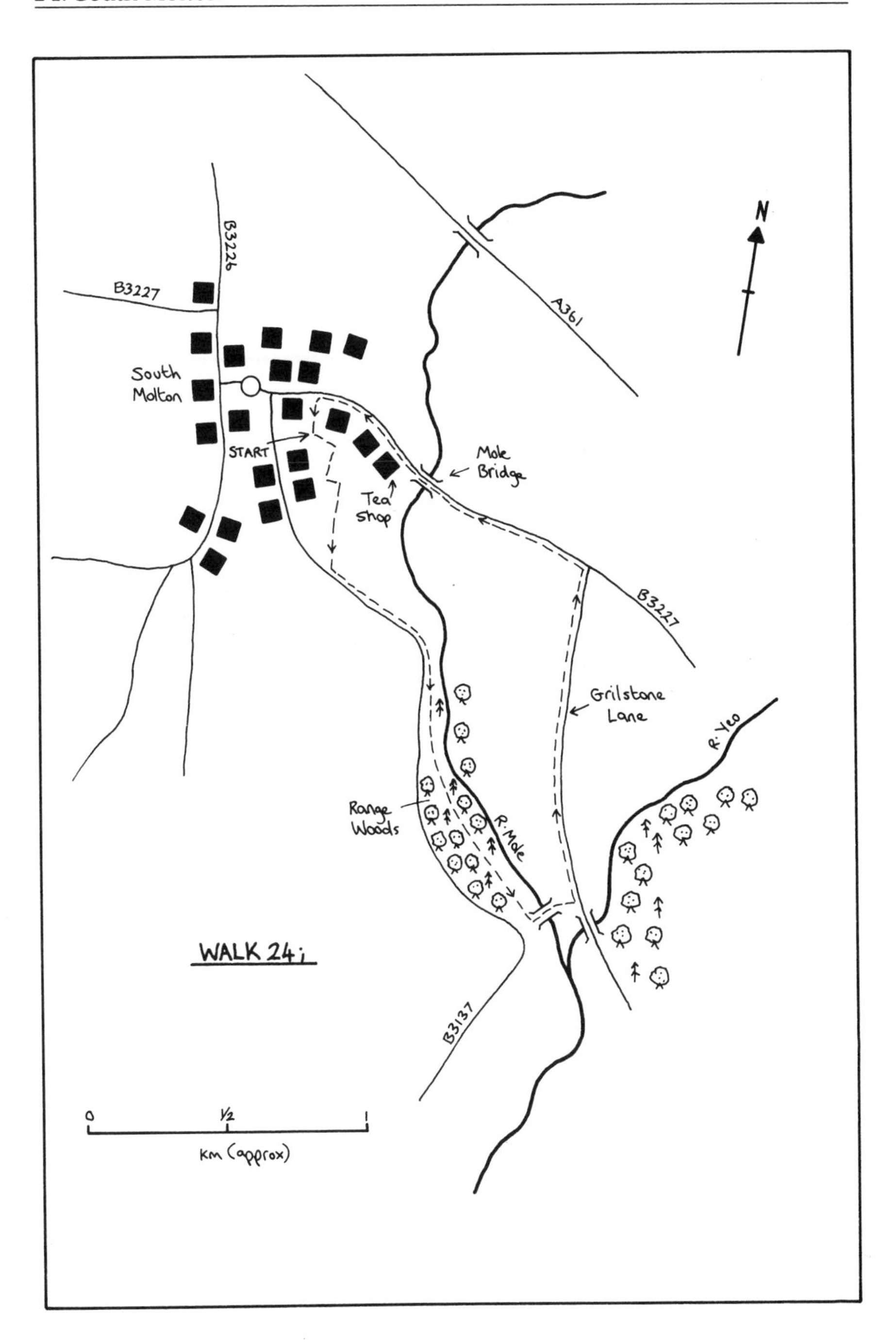
B3226
B3227
South Molton
START
Tea shop
Mole Bridge
A361
N
B3227
Grilstone Lane
R. Yeo
Range Woods
R. Mole
B3137
WALK 24:
0
½
1
Km (approx)

25. Chulmleigh and Chawleigh

Length: 6¼ miles (10km)

Summary: Another circular walk through the countryside of deepest rural Devon connecting a small town and a big village. Partly on minor roads and partly on right of way footpaths and byways which seem to be little used. Consequently, there is a certain amount of care needed in route finding and a fair amount of rough ground underfoot The route lies largely in the attractive valley of the Little Dart River, nothing to do with the better known rivers flowing south from Dartmoor. There are considerable rises and falls up and down the sides of the valley.

Car Parking: Free designated parking spaces on either side of the church in Chulmleigh. Grid reference 686141/2.

Map: Ordnance Survey Landranger no. 180, Barnstaple and Ilfracombe area, 1:50,000.

The Tea Shop

For morning coffee, brunch, lunch, or afternoon tea, The Old Bakehouse in Chulmleigh can be highly recommended. Holly and Colin Burls run this establishment in a friendly and efficient manner. Local foods such as Devonshire braised lamb or Dartmouth kippers, Colin's pasta bake, or Holly's Surprise – a filled savoury pancake, are all very tempting dishes; there is also the Bakehouse Brunch or Devon cream tea. These are just some of the items from the attractive menu. Accommodation also available; evening meals by arrangement only. Open: 10.30am – 4pm, Tuesday to Saturday (closed on Monday). Sunday, 12.30 – 4pm for traditional roast lunch and afternoon teas only. These hours apply all the year but The Old Bakehouse may be closed for a few weeks for holidays in the winter months – just check by 'phone. Tel: 01769 580137

Old water pump, Chulmleigh

About the area

Chulmleigh is a charming little town with narrow streets and thatched buildings clustering close to the parish church of St Mary Magdalene with its impressive 15th century tower. Inside the church there is a particularly good screen and there are angels in the roof. Look for the pre-conquest roundel over the south door. The Barnstaple Inn is more than 300 years old and has a claimed connection with King Charles I. Separated from its bigger neighbour by the deep valley of the Little Dart River, Chawleigh is a spaced out village with the 15th century church of St James as its best feature. Worth seeing are the 15th century rood screen and an unusual lych gate.

The Walk

From the church, walk to the main street in Chulmleigh, reached at one end. At a junction ignore a road dropping very steeply to the right and bear left along a level road, passing Davy Park. Go straight on at the next junction and leave town on the surfaced lane, gently downhill. A 1 in 4 length of road drops abruptly to the valley bottom.

Cross a considerable stream over a 'weak bridge', pass Park Mill and, before the road rises, turn right a gate with a 'public footpath' sign. The route lies close to the fence on the right, well trodden by cattle if not by humans. Go over a waymarked stile, a bridge over an obvious former leat, and then another bridge on the right. There is no real track across the next meadow. Take a straight line across to a wide opening in the hedge and continue across the next field.

Towards the end of the next, long, meadow bear right to cross the Little Dart River on a footbridge. Cross a plantation of young conifers, bearing a little right, and enter the woodland. In a few metres there is an obvious track rising to the right. Follow this uphill, soon bending left Go straight on upwards at a vague junction. The track is good, terracing up the valley side through attractive woodland.

Leave the wood at a farm gate, heading for a second gate. An inviting farm track heads away to the left before this second gate but, according to the Ordnance Survey, this is not a right of way; the correct line is to go right at this point, looping back left in a short dis-

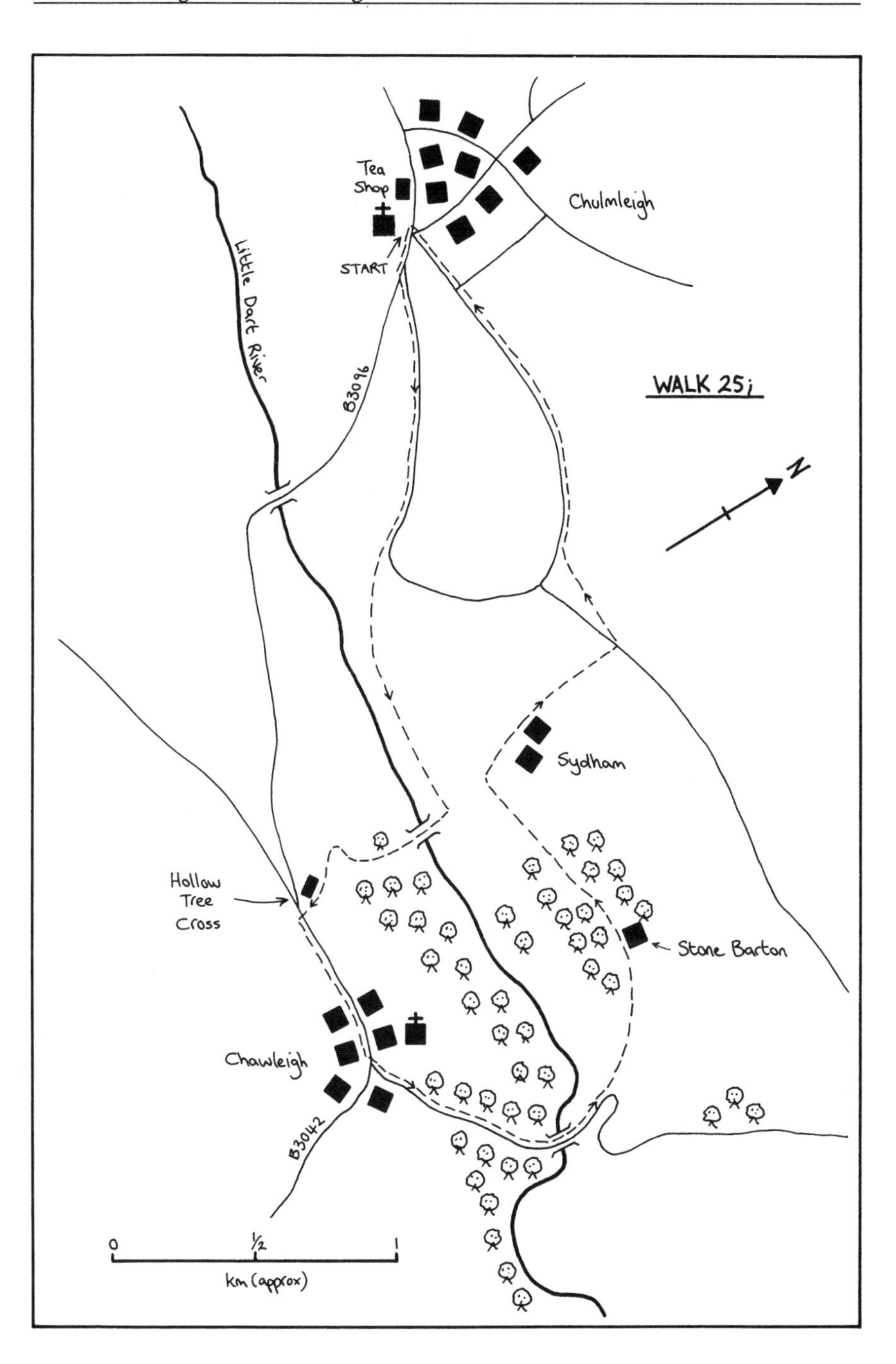

Tea Shop
START
Chulmleigh
Little Dart River
B3096
WALK 25i
N
Sydham
Hollow Tree Cross
Stone Barton
Chawleigh
B3042
0
½
1
km (approx)

tance. The obvious farm track keeps above a small wooded valley before reaching the public road by Hollow Tree Cross.

The Ordnance Survey right of way cuts back across the farm track to reach the road on the other (i.e. Chawleigh) side of the building at Hollow Tree Cross. Turn left to walk along the road to Chawleigh. On approaching the church, go either right to pass the inn or left, signposted 'toilets'.

After the church turn left to descend the valley side on a very minor road, quite acceptable for walkers. Cross the river by Stone Mill, turning left towards 'Gidley Arms 5' As the road bends very sharply to the right, go along a concrete driveway heading for Stone Barton Farm, rising nicely across the valley side, with Chulmleigh church soon in view. Go through the farm complex on the roadway. To the right, above, is the site of an ancient fortification.

At the far end of the farm bear a little left into a slightly sunken bridleway at the upper edge of woodland, going gently downhill. This is basically a good, if little-used, track. Go through two gates to cross another track and continue the same line. Cross a tiny stream and go through a gate into an open meadow.

Cross the meadow to a gate on the far side. Sydham Farm is above to the right. Continue for a further 100m and then bend right, uphill, through a narrow belt of woodland, rather muddy underfoot. Reach the concrete farm access roadway and go straight across, through or over an old gate with a faded waymark to continue along the same sort of track, between hedges, up to the public road.

Cross to a 'public footpath' sign and go over the fence. This is a road-avoiding short cut descending across fields but without much evidence of a path on the ground. Bear left to reach the exit gate at the bottom left corner. Rejoin the road and turn right, crossing a stream before the final uphill return to Chulmleigh. Reach the main street at a junction and turn right to walk to the tea shop.

26. Eggesford

Length: 3 miles (4.8km)

Summary: A varied circuit including Forest Enterprises woodland and upland farming country, with interesting features, close to the valley of the River Taw. Generally good underfoot apart from a small section of path churned by farming activity. The walk is based on the Eggesford Country Centre complex.

Car Parking: At Eggesford Country Centre. Grid reference 110685.

Map: Ordnance Survey Landranger no. 191, Okehampton and North Dartmoor area, 1:50,000.

The Tea Shop

The Garden Restaurant at Eggesford Garden Centre appears deceptively unattractive from the car park and it is difficult to find the entrance! Don't be put off – go into the garden shop and follow the cardboard tea-pot signs suspended from the ceiling. From the elevated tea room there are pleasant views of the Taw Valley whilst outside are tables on a sheltered terrace; there is also an open balcony for sunny days. Good selection of food and beverages available ranging from cooked meals to ice creams. Try the lemon shortcake with afternoon tea. Prices are very reasonable. Open: every day 9.30am – 6pm summer and until 5pm in winter all the year except Christmas and New Year holidays. Tel: 01769 580250

About the area

Deep in the quiet valley of the River Taw, Eggesford is hardly worth calling a hamlet, let alone a village. But – it does have a railway station with services to Exeter and Barnstaple; it does have extensive woodlands which include the first ever plantings by the former Forestry Commission; it does have the Eggesford Country Centre and it is now much promoted as 'Tarka' country as the Taw Valley was very much part of the territory of Henry Williamson's famous otter.

All in all, an area ideal for gentle walking and exploration. The large estate which included Eggesford was based on Eggesford House, originally of 1620. This early house was replaced in 1828-32 by the present house which was unfortunately vacated in 1911 and has since steadily become more derelict. The ruin, on high ground, can be seen from the Country Centre and from part of the route of the walk.

The railway along the Taw valley, connecting Exeter and Barnstaple, was built by the great engineer Sir Thomas Brassey and opened in 1854. It became part of the London and South Western Railway (later the Southern Railway) in 1863. As the only surviving line to the important town of Barnstaple, it has been spared the massive branch line closures of the 1950s and 60s. It is now referred to as the 'Tarka' line. The Eggesford Country Centre comprises a commercial garden centre, substantial refreshment catering, a small information/local history section, cycle hire and organised trails in the nearby forest. Eggesford church has monuments to the Chichester family, owners of the estate for many years.

The Walk

From the Country Centre walk down to the lower car park and turn right, along a well made path, soon descending to join a surfaced lane. Turn right, towards the church. Go through the gate beside the church, noting the 'Tarka Trail' sign. Follow a stony drive, going straight ahead at a three-way sign, rising steadily. By the entrance to the Eggesford Barton complex turn right to stay outside the perimeter fence.

The track continues unmistakably along the edge of a prairie-sized field, churned by tractor wheels in places. There are long views back over the Taw Valley and across to the sad ruin of Eggesford House. The occasional stile and waymark reassures us that we are still with the Tarka Trail.

On reaching a public road at Eggesford Fourways, with a war memorial, go straight ahead for Brushford and Winkley. In about 300m turn right at the second of two adjacent farm gates, with 'public footpath' sign. At first there is no apparent path but keep close to the fence on the right. In 100m go right through a small gate and descend through the mixed woodland of the Hayne Valley on a well defined

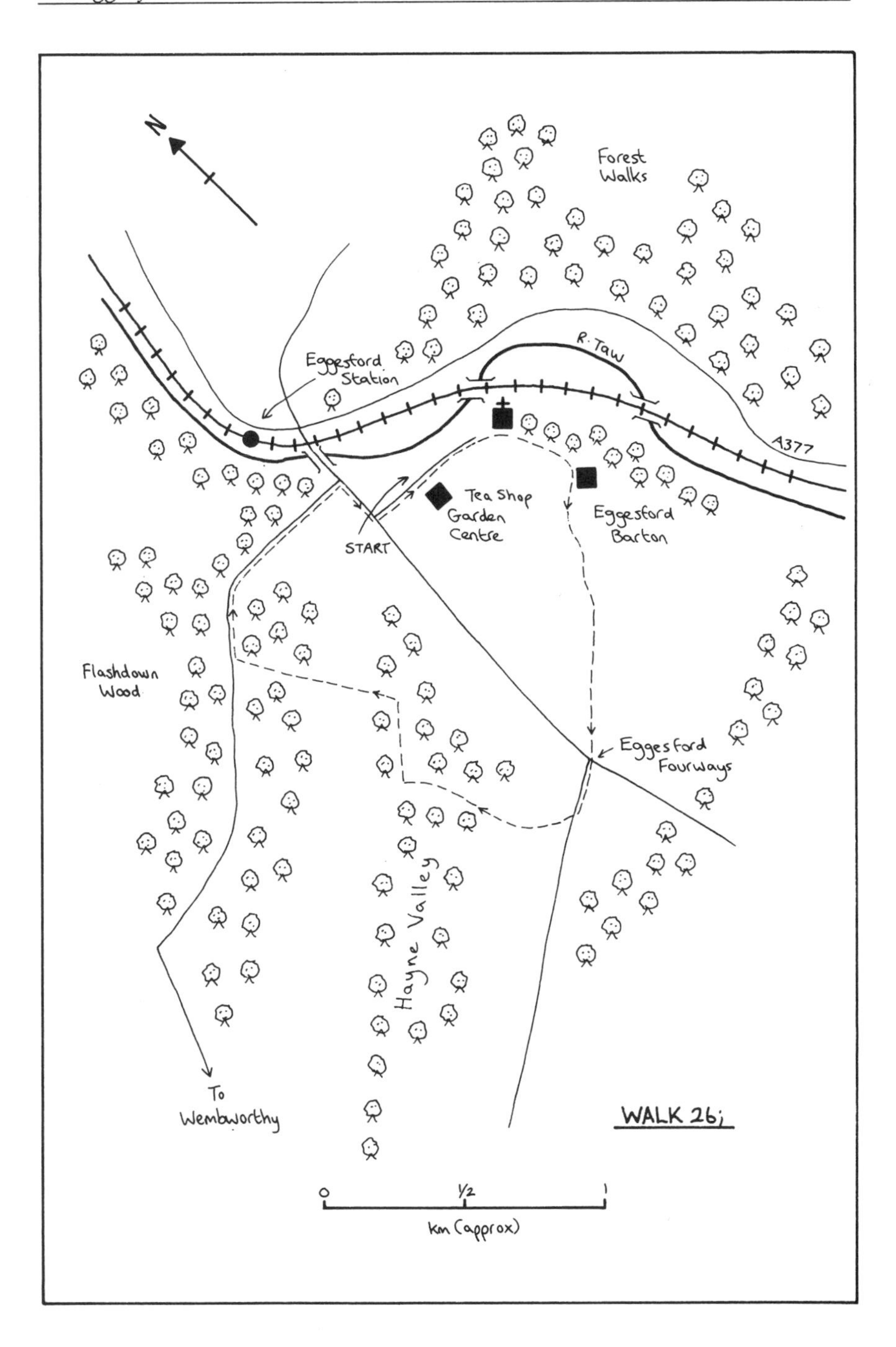
N
Forest Walks
R. Taw
Eggesford Station
A377
Tea Shop
Garden Centre
Eggesford Barton
START
Flashdown Wood
Eggesford Fourways
Hayne Valley
To Wembworthy
WALK 26;
0
1/2
1
km (approx)

The Taw Valley, Eggesford

path. Bluebells, foxgloves and other wild flowers line the track which soon becomes a forest roadway. At a major junction turn right, down to a gate.

In about 400m a public bridleway crosses the forest roadway. There is no signpost but turn left here, steeply up a stony track. Note that the enticing continuation of the roadway leads only to a padlocked and barbed wire festooned gate! The bridleway is obviously used frequently by horses, one section being quite hoof-churned. Pass the entrance to Scrabba Cleave House and shortly enter Flashdown Wood. In 100m, at a clearing, divert right along an avenue of beech trees to a plaque on the right recording the planting, on 8th December, 1969, of trees to commemorate the 50th anniversary of the first planting by the Forestry Commission. In a further 100m another plaque on an upright stone commemorates the first ever Forestry Commission planting, here on 8th December, 1919. Return to the route, go to the public road and turn right to descend, in half a mile, to the junction at Cott Cross. Turn right, rise for 50m, and turn left to return to the Country Centre.

27. Hatherleigh Moor

Length: 4 miles (6.4km)

Summary: A walk to and from the centre of an attractive little old market town, with a circuit of Hatherleigh Moor. Generally easy walking but with an ascent along the road out of town and some rough grass on the moor.

Car Parking: Large free car park by the cattle market in Hatherleigh. Grid reference 540043.

Map: Ordnance Survey Landranger no. 191, Okehampton and North Dartmoor area, 1:50,000.

The Tea Shop

The Acorns tea room appears to be popular with local people and is particularly busy on market days when Devonians from miles around converge on Hatherleigh. Since our visit, there has been a change of ownership. Mrs Mann, the enthusiastic new proprietor, confirms that a comprehensive menu will be served; all the food including cakes and scones, is home-made and that vegetarian dishes are available. Every Sunday a traditional roast lunch will be served and reservations for this are accepted. It is anticipated that the cafe will be open every day all the year from 8 am to 5 pm. If in any doubt, just telephone 01837 810479

About the area

Hatherleigh is a generally quiet traditional small market town with a long history, two 15th century inns, the George being the more striking, and the mainly 15th century church of St John the Baptist. The church has barrel roofs, with angels, and a Norman font. The right to hold a market was first bestowed in the 10th century by the Abbots

Sculpture at Hatherleigh market

of Tavistock and, to the present day, Tuesday is the great day for Hatherleigh.

The cattle and general markets, part indoors part outdoors, jostle together in the most natural way for a country town, with a strong emphasis on local produce. The town comes vigorously to life as the voice of the auctioneer carries easily to the town centre and the narrow streets are filled with the hustle and bustle of the local farming community.

Hatherleigh Pottery, in Market Street, allows visitors to see work in progress around a beautiful cobbled courtyard. There is a shop/showroom and a tourist information display. Hatherleigh Moor is an unusual expanse of semi-improved grassland, much of it now rush dominated, extending to about 500 acres. It was given to the inhabitants of Hatherleigh in the 14th century by the Abbotts of Tavistock. The local householders ('potboilers') have rights to graze stock and to gather furze (gorse) for fuel.

St John's Well on the moor is reputed to have been consecrated as a 'holy well' at the same time as the parish church. From the moor the Buddle stream flows underground to emerge in the High Street as pure drinking water. There was a minor Civil War battle on the moor in 1644. After ploughing for the first time during World War II, the moor is now less rich in the formerly diverse plant species and there has been some recent diversion of the old rights of way.

On the north eastern fringe the Hatherleigh Monument, a large obelisk, commemorates Colonel William Morris, a local member of the 17th Lancers, who took part in the Charge of the Light Brigade in 1850.

The Walk

Pass the farmers, sheep and dog sculpture and turn right at the main street – Bridge Street – to pass the modern Methodist church. Turn sharp left into South Street and rise steadily. Go straight across at a cross roads into Victoria Street, still rising, to reach Stone Cross, with its well worn ancient cross. Continue until the moor is obvious on the right. One hundred and fifty metres past the last house on the right go through a farm gate with a 'public bridleway Tarka Trail' sign. The track is hardly marked on the grass, but follow the line indicated by the signpost, aiming for a gate by a tree. The long views are across to Dartmoor, including its highest point, High Wilhays 621m (2038ft). Continue the same line after the gate, a little left of that indicated by the signpost. The Hatherleigh Monument is visible to the left.

By another signpost cross a tiny valley with willow trees, to a gate. Go ahead to the left of a little clump of trees eventually reaching a fence at a defunct signpost, where the previous line of the right of way has obviously been obstructed. Turn left along the line of the fence to a signposted gate close to a minor road. There are early purple orchids in several places on the moor. Keep close to the road until a fence forces a right turn towards the far end of a wooded area. Stay with the fence, raking back left to a double 'bridleway' signpost which is at the end of a short lane.

Take the line indicated by the nearer of the two signs, diverging from the woodland on the left. At first there is no obvious path but a worn track is found some way on. The line is just south of west. There are two signposts along the way which confirm the correct line. At the second signpost go straight on, then round a cattle pen to a small gate on to a minor road. Turn right. This quiet road provides a good route back into Hatherleigh along the edge of the moor.

Reach the top end of Higher Street and go across the junction into High Street. Turn left at a more major street – Bridge Street. The Acorn tea room is on the right. Turn right by the Spar shop to return to the car park.

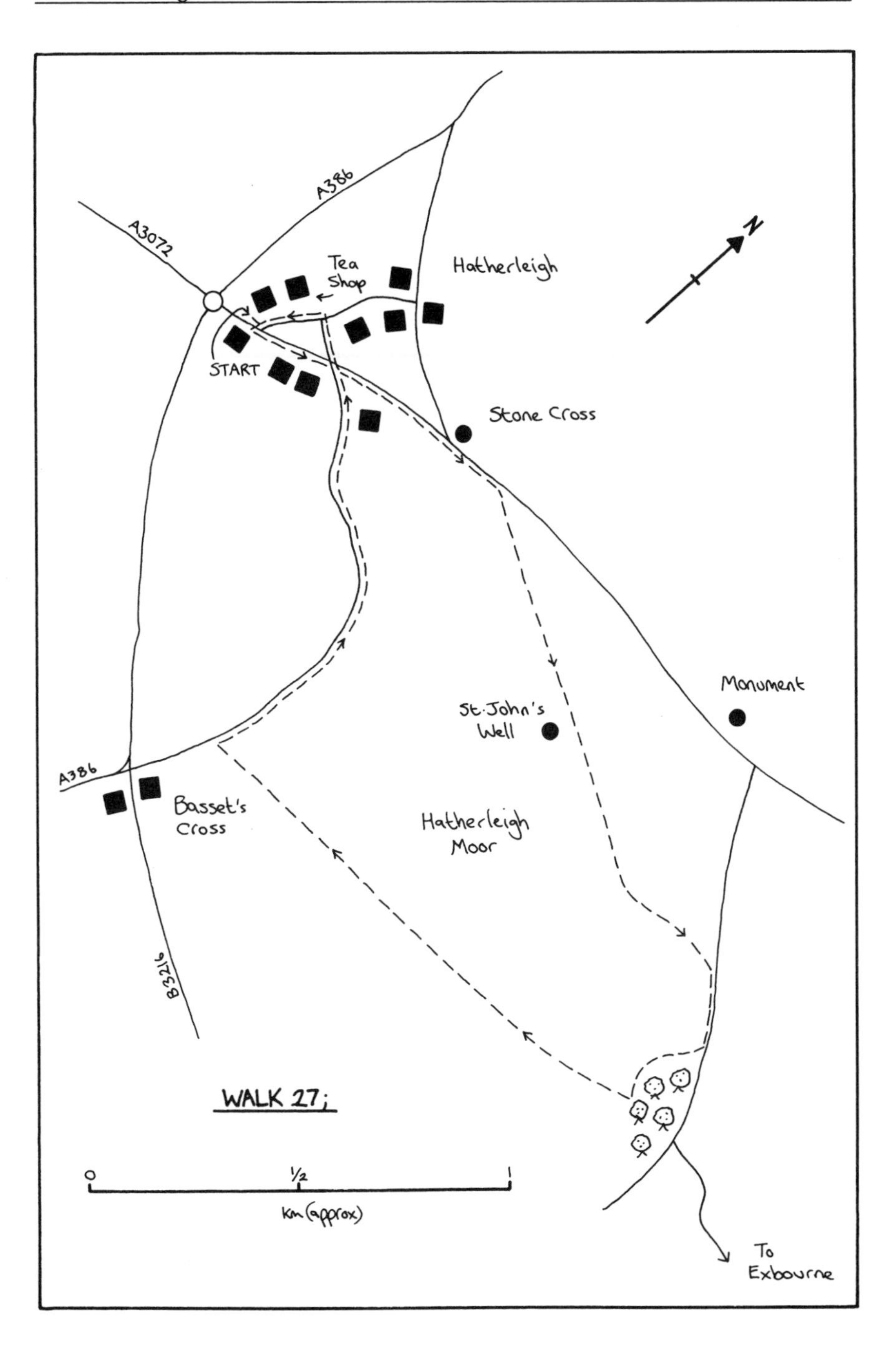

A386
A3072
Tea Shop
Hatherleigh
N
START
Stone Cross
Monument
St. John's Well
A386
Basset's Cross
Hatherleigh Moor
B3216
WALK 27;
0
½
1
Km (approx)
To Exbourne

28. Okehampton and East Hill

Length: 3½ miles (5.6km); short version 2¾ miles (4.4km); to include town, 4 miles (6.4km)

Summary: A circuit based on the newly renovated Okehampton station, combining the fine high viewpoint of East Hill (350m – 1149ft) with an attractive section of the East Okement River. Although never far from Okehampton, the route does provide a genuine country walk, mainly on good footpaths. The ascent of East Hill is quite long but not excessively steep. The standard and shorter versions avoid contact with the town centre, whilst the long version includes the centre, with alternative refreshment possibilities.

Car Parking: Enlarged car park by renovated railway station. Grid reference 592945. Gates locked at 6.30pm.

Map: Ordnance Survey Outdoor Leisure no. 28, Dartmoor, 1:25,000 or Landranger no. 191, Okehampton and North Devon area, 1:50,000.

The Tea Shop

Railway enthusiasts will know that Oliver Bulleid is an important name in railway history. He was Chief Engineer for the Southern Railway from the mid 1930s to late forties. His name lives on! – the tea shop here at Okehampton Station, the Bulleid Buffet, is appropriately named after this famous man. Indeed everything about the menu is "railway" too. Visitors are invited to "fuel-up" before the walk or to "re-fuel" afterwards! Food offered includes such robust fare as cheesy chuffer cheeseburger, porter's pasty, wheel-tapper's steak and kidney pie, engine driver's bacon butty, and others too. For something lighter, there are salads, cream teas, ices, coffee, tea, and cold drinks. Decor is in Southern Region colours of green and cream and the furniture is attractive and in character. There are tables on the platform under the canopy. The whole complex is smart

Okehampton Station and Buffet

with delightful tubs of flowers and hanging baskets. Open: every day – May to October, 9.30am – 5pm; November to April, 10.30am – 4.30pm. There are special events held during the Christmas period. Tel: 01837 55330.

Should the walker prefer to visit Okehampton town centre "Le Café Noir" in Red Lion Yard is recommended. Very good selection of food here from Danish pastries, toasted sandwiches, coffees, teas, through to full meals. Ignore the French name – full English breakfasts are served all day! The decor is superb with a French /Continental atmosphere in a courtyard setting. The black and white tiled floor, good lighting, cane chairs, all add to the "feel-good-factor". Open: 9.30am to 4.30pm every day all the year – closed on Sundays Tel: 0183754234

About the area

The largest town for many miles around, sitting close below the northern edge of Dartmoor, Okehampton was long notorious as one of the great West Country traffic bottlenecks. Now relieved of that problem it has again become quite a nice old town, with plenty of shops, inns, cafés and restaurants. The modern precinct which includes 'Café Noir' is attractive.

There is plenty of interest for the visitor in Okehampton. The old castle, by the Exeter road, was dismantled by order of King Henry VIII and has been in ruins ever since. The town hall was originally built as a house in 1685, being converted to municipal use in 1821. The Museum of Dartmoor Life is also centrally situated, in an early 19th century mill just off West Street. Strong on local history, arts and crafts, with interactive exhibits and a working waterwheel, the museum also houses a shop for gifts and books, tourist information and small scale catering. A well laid out town trail links these and many other features. A leaflet is obtainable at the tourist information centre.

A more recent development may be found at the railway station, where a visitor centre is being created. The railway arrived in Okehampton in October 1871 as an extension of the London and South Western Railway's line from Exeter, eventually reaching Padstow in Cornwall as the terminus of a through line from London Waterloo. The line grew in importance, many trains being divided at Okehampton into sections for Plymouth and for North Cornwall. After the line was taken over by the Southern Railway, there were important through trains such as the Atlantic Coast Express. One of Bulleid's post World War II 'West Country' class Light Pacific locomotives was named 'Okehampton' in a ceremony at the station. Following the Beeching report, the Cornwall lines closed in 1966, followed by the Plymouth services in 1968. Finally, in 1972, the Exeter to Okehampton service terminated. Fortunately, because of freight traffic from Meldon Quarry, the lines remained in use, although the station buildings became increasingly dilapidated. From 1994, imaginative plans have been prepared by a partnership of official and other bodies. These plans will bring the station and other former railway buildings back into productive use in a phased programme. The station has already been restored in a 1930s – 50s style and colour scheme, with buffet, model shop and railway museum, whilst the old goods shed will be a youth hostel. But, wonder of wonders, in 1997 a passenger train service to and from Exeter was reinstated on summer Sundays, with linking bus services at Okehampton. Presumably this is an experiment which will continue only if there is sufficient support.

The Walk

Pass the station buildings to reach the public road and turn left under the railway line, signposted 'footpath East Hill. Klondyke Corner'. Follow the surfaced road steeply uphill between high banks. At a four-way sign, go ahead to follow 'footpath', through a gate to Heathfield House. Pass the house and go through a little gate. The footpath next leads to an impressive footbridge over the A30, Okehampton by-pass.

On the other side turn right and then left to follow tracks worn in the grass of a huge rising meadow, the objective being the top left hand corner. Go over a stile to join a road. Continue up the road for 100m, then turn left to a signpost offering two routes for walkers Cross the cattle grid and bear left over grass to the top of East Hill, with triangulation point. The views are extensive; over Okehampton to the north and towards high Dartmoor, including Belstone Tors, to the south and south east. An army camp is prominent to the south west. Lower Halstock Farm is to the right, below.

Continue along the broad ridge. There is no definite path but the close cropped grass, between clumps of gorse, offers good walking and this is 'Access Land'. On approaching an old wall/bank, bear left to follow it closely, turning right as the wall turns right.

There are now more definite paths, descending quite steeply through woodland into the valley of Moor Brook. Any will suffice to reach the valley bottom, but the best is probably a narrow path which bends left to stay on the valley side, about 20m above an old stone wall which is close to the lively rushing brook. The path soon descends to the valley bottom, becoming broader and clearer as it approaches the confluence with the East Okement River, close to a footbridge.

Don't cross, but bear left along a broad riverside path, easy going but with one stony section. The woodland is well diversified, oak, ash, silver birch and holly. At a three-way signpost go straight on for 'Okehampton', under the A30 viaduct. Next is the railway viaduct, with another signpost.

At the signpost the short route turns left – 'bridlepath to Station Road'. This path stays above the river on its direct route back to the station, with its own gate into the station yard.

For the main route turn right at the signpost, over a footbridge, signposted 'Okehampton via Ball Hill'. Go under the viaduct, through a gate and pass a bungalow to reach a surfaced roadway. In less than 50m turn left at a signpost 'Okehampton via Ball Hill'. Go through a gate and follow the excellent path along the valley side, accompanied for much of the way by the long leat which served the Town Mills.

The way is entirely straightforward to follow until it reaches a surfaced road by a school. *To add the town centre to the walk go straight ahead here, then follow Mill Road to the left, passing the entrance to Simmons Park. Bear right into St James Street, then left through The Arcade. Red Lion Yard, with the Café Noir tea rooms is across the main street. Return to Simmons Park and take the well-used path alongside the river, eventually rising to the right, then turning right to pass between properties to Station Road. Turn left to return to the station.*

For the standard route turn left by the school, pass the car park and go through a gate into the school playing fields. Keep close to the hedge on the left, pass Okehampton Town football club, cross a children's play area and then a bridge over the river. Ascend the steep valley side on steps, fork left, and carry on up to Station Road. Turn left to return to the station and the car park.

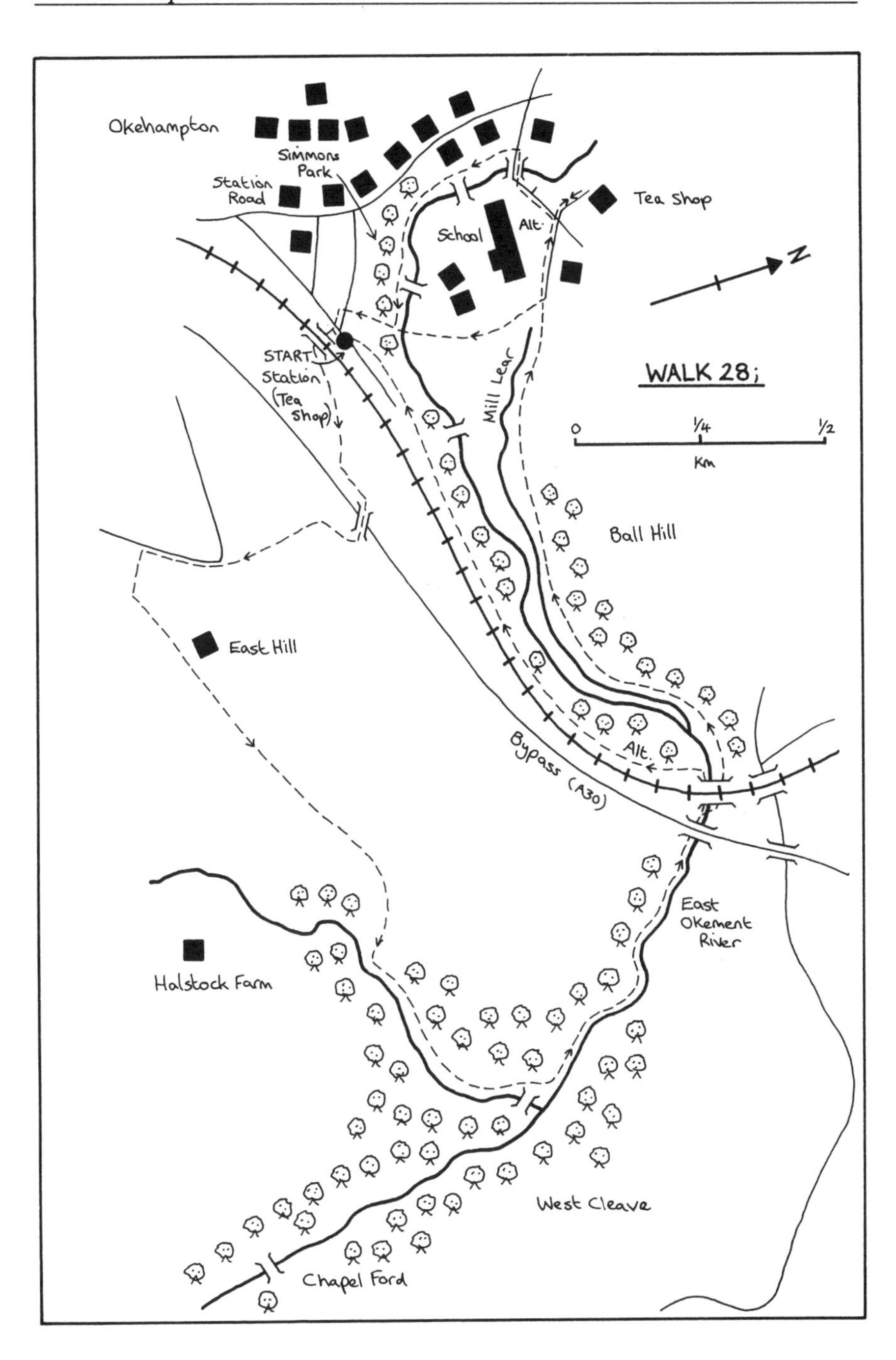

Okehampton
Simmons Park
Station Road
Tea Shop
School
Alt.
N
START
Station (Tea Shop)
Mill Lear
WALK 28;
0
1/4
1/2
Km
Ball Hill
East Hill
Alt.
Bypass (A30)
East Okement River
Halstock Farm
West Cleave
Chapel Ford

29. Belstone and Sticklepath

Length: 3¾ miles (6km)

Summary: A highly recommended walk up and down Belstone Cleave, a lovely part of the upper valley of the River Taw, here fresh from its rising high on Dartmoor. There is little rise and fall and most of the tracks used are fine, with just a little mud and some stony sections.

Car Parking: Substantial free car park by the northern edge of Belstone village. Grid reference 621938.

Map: Ordnance Survey Outdoor Leisure no. 28, Dartmoor, 1:25,000 or Landranger no. 191, Okehampton and North Dartmoor area, 1:50,000.

The Tea Shop

The Round House Café is constructed of timber and is completely in harmony with its surroundings at Finch Foundry. Attractive but small – only four or five tables indoors, there is plenty of seating outside. Obviously not a large menu on offer here but perfectly adequate. Items sampled were of good quality and the service was friendly. Open: 11 – 5pm daily (closed on Tuesdays) from April(or Easter) to end of October approx. Note: This National Trust café is fully accessible to the public; it can be visited without paying admission charge to tour the foundry. Tel: 01837 840046

About the area

Sticklepath Forge, operated as the Finch Foundry from early in the 19th century until closure in 1960, is powered by three water wheels using water from the River Taw. Inside, an amazing array of Victorian machinery, including tilt hammers, grinders and forges, was used to make shovels, sickles and scythes for agriculture and mining. Now in the care of the National Trust, as a museum of rural in-

Sticklepath Forge waterwheel

dustry, the forge has working demonstrations of some of the machinery, still operated by the original water power. A tea pavilion and picnic area have been added at the rear.

Adjacent to the Forge, a Quaker 'burying' ground has a peaceful site by the river.

Sticklepath village has a post office/store but little else of interest. However, John Wesley did preach here frequently, from the white rock on the hillside at the Okehampton end of the village.

An edge of Dartmoor village, sitting above the infant River Taw, Belstone is quietly pretty. The church has a fine altarpiece and a Norman font. Both the 'Tarka Trail' and the 'Two Museums Trail' run along Belstone Cleave.

The Walk

Walk through Belstone village, keeping left to reach what appears to be a common grazing area. There is a small gravelled area on the left. Follow a track faintly worn over the grass here, descending to a seat. The path becomes more obvious and stony as it drops towards the River Taw, bending sharp left at a wet section.

Cross the river by a footbridge and keep left along a cattle-pounded track with an old wall close on the left. Keep left at each of two forks to stay as close as possible to the river. Although the path is initially rather rough it does improve as progress is made. The valley is very attractive, with some exposed rocks high on the sides (to qualify for the title 'cleave'?) and the bottom is richly vegetated, with rhododendron prominent.

The path roughens again before a three-way signpost is reached. Turn left to cross the river on a footbridge, signposted 'Skaigh'. Rise to turn right on another path parallel with the river, soon reaching another three-way signpost. Turn right for 'Sticklepath' and slant left to cross the river on another footbridge.

A delightful riverside path now heads for Sticklepath; this is real 'Tarka the Otter' country, with the sound of the waters ever present. Pass an old dam and go over a stile as civilisation is approached. At a junction with three-way signpost turn left for 'Sticklepath and A30 road'. In 100m turn left over a footbridge, signposted to 'Museum of

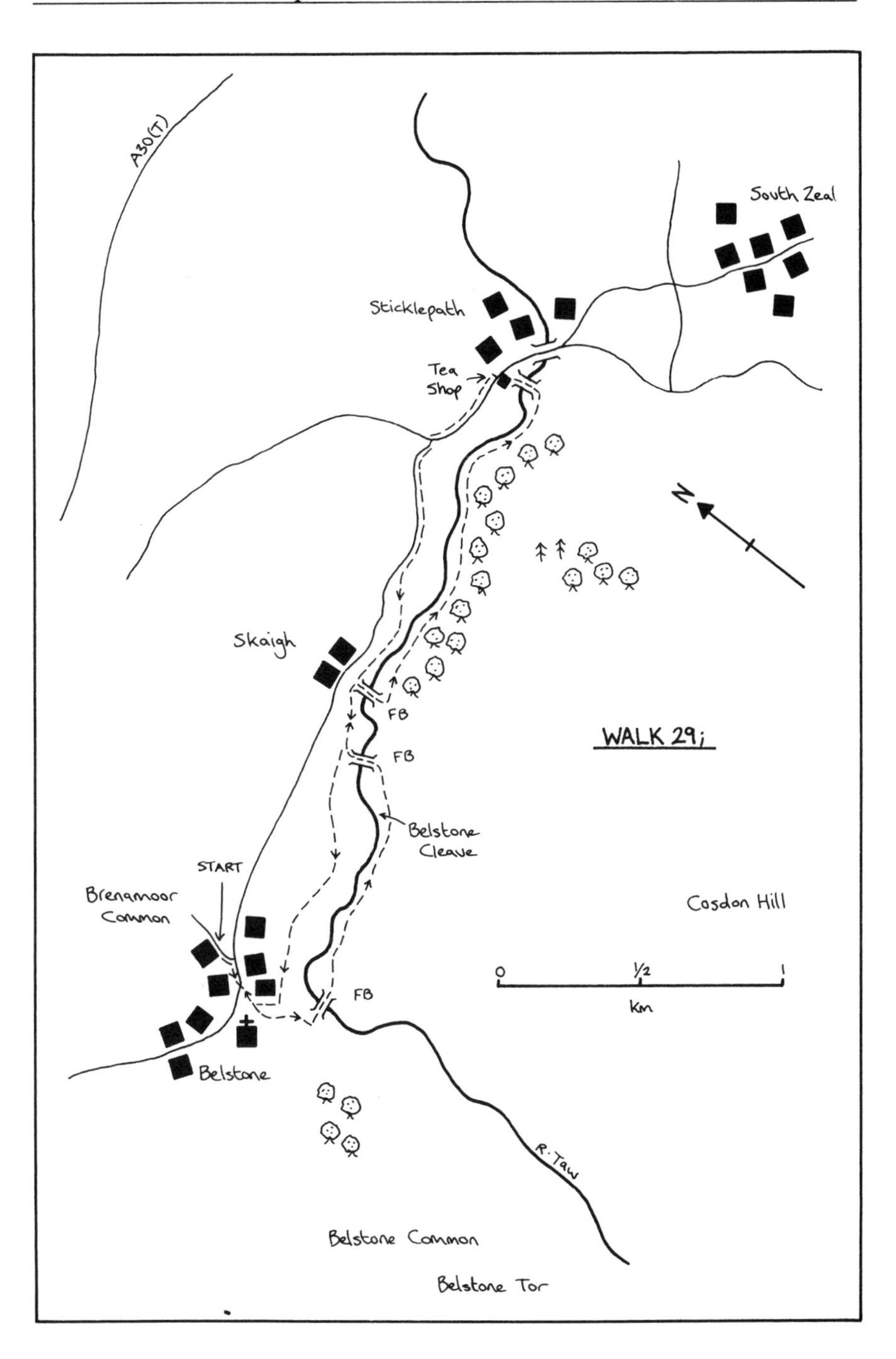
A30(T)
South Zeal
Sticklepath
Tea Shop
Skaigh
FB
FB
WALK 29;
Belstone Cleave
START
Brenamoor Common
Cosdon Hill
0
½
1
Km
FB
Belstone
R. Taw
Belstone Common
Belstone Tor

Water Power' and cross the Taw yet again to reach the car park of the Finch Foundry, with the Round House café, the Quaker Burying Ground and an interesting 19th century summerhouse behind.

To return, from the foundry turn left along the main street as far as the first road junction, by the site of the former Lady Well. Turn left along a minor road 'Skaigh ½ mile'. This attractive little road stays close to the river. Before reaching Skaigh bear left along a good track with two signposts. Follow 'Belstone, waymarked path and the Moor'. The excellent track continues through the woodland of the Cleave. At a three-way signpost keep straight on for 'Belstone and the Moor'. One muddy section of path has been roughly stoned. The track eventually climbs to the right, up the valley side and there are long views to part of Dartmoor including the jagged top of Belstone Tors.

Join another path and turn left, along the top edge of the valley, with an old wall close on the right. Rejoin the outward route on grazing land and turn right to return through the village to the car park.

30. Knightshayes Court

Length: 1 mile

Summary: A gentle amble around a numbered nature trail, The Impey Walk, in the woodland adjacent to the National Trust owned Knightshayes Court. Entirely straightforward but there is a modest uphill section. Walking boots are not really necessary although there is a little mud. The walk may readily be combined with a visit to the gardens and/or the house.

Car Parking: Series of organised car parks used for visitors to the house. Typical grid reference 961155.

Map: Ordnance Survey Landranger no. 181, Minehead and Brendon Hills area, 1:50,000.

The Tea Shop

The Stables Tea Room – obviously housed in the converted stables - even has the original floor complete with drainage system! However, all is now very hygienic and attractive. The furniture is in keeping with the surroundings and the pleasant ladies serving food at the counter wear Victorian dresses and aprons. A good selection of hot and cold food is served all day. The home-made soup proved to be excellent. There's a choice of cakes, ice cream, and the usual range of drinks plus one or two less usual ones such as elderflower pressé. Open: Easter or 1st April to end of October 11am - 4.30pm everyday but closed on Fridays except Good Friday Tel: 01884 254665

About the area

Knightshayes Court was constructed between 1869 and 1874, for John Heathcoat-Amory, Member of Parliament for Tiverton. The designer was William Burges. The house remained in the Heathcoat-Amory family until the second Sir John died in 1972, leaving the property to the National Trust. Some of the Victorian room decoration has been restored by the Trust and the contents of the house include family portraits, a collection of Old Masters and much of the family furniture and china.

The gardens extend to 50 acres, largely created in the present century, but based on the original landscaping done by Edward Kemp. Much re-planning and planting were carried out in the 1950s, so successfully that Sir John and Lady Heathcoat Amory were awarded the Victoria Medal of Horticulture by the Royal Horticultural Society. The different parts of the garden are distinctively separated. Notable are the conservatory, the terraces, the pool garden and the Fox and Hounds topiary. The Douglas Fir Walk is quite different; the massive specimens of this North American tree were planted in the 1870s and are now among the tallest in the country. Inhabitants of the woodland include badgers, grey squirrels and rabbits. Quiet walkers may also see foxes, red deer and roe deer.

The former stable now houses the shop and restaurant. Outside, a good array of plants is available for purchase by visitors.

The Walk

At the far end of the first car park there is a prominent 'Impey Walk' signpost. Start here, enter the woods and follow the excellent footpath progressively from post 1 to post 9. The official leaflet describing the walk may be purchased from the reception area/shop in the stables block. One of the salient features of the walk is the rich diversity of the trees, many being quite recent plantings to replace damage caused during a great storm in 1990.

In the early part of the walk there are good views to the left across farming countryside to Allers Farm. The stream in front of the farm is called Town Leat. From as early as 1250, water from this stream was conducted for 5 miles into Tiverton as the town supply. After passing a fine Wellingtonia tree, modern waterworks can be seen to the left, followed by the farming hamlet of Chettiscombe, part of the Knightshayes estate and roughly contemporary with Knightshayes Court.

From close to the highest part of the walk are the longest views;

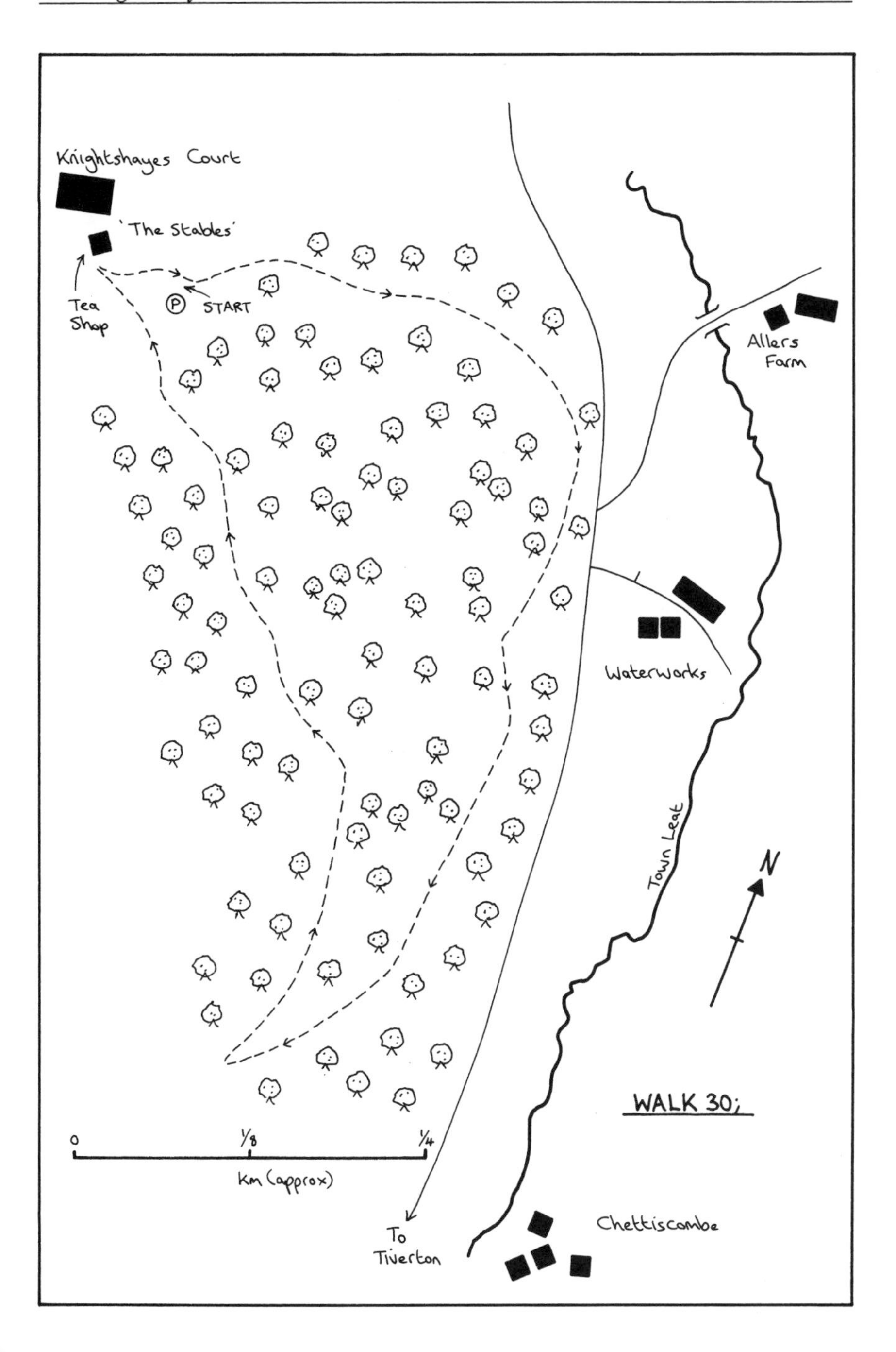
Knightshayes Court
'The Stables'
Tea Shop
START
P
Allers Farm
Waterworks
Town Leat
N
WALK 30;
0
1/8
1/4
Km (approx)
To Tiverton
Chettiscombe

Garden at Knightshayes

nearby is Chettiscombe, but on a clear day the geological fault of Sidmouth Gap on the south coast is visible on the horizon. Towards the end of the walk is a plantation of western hemlocks which were grown to provide a windbreak for the garden. The path emerges above the car parks. Continue to the stable block for refreshments.